Excel 5 for Windows
The Visual Learning Guide

Watch for these forthcoming titles in this series:

WINFAX PRO for Windows: The Visual Learning Guide
Ami Pro for Windows: The Visual Learning Guide
PowerPoint for Windows: The Visual Learning Guide

Available Now!

Windows 3.1: The Visual Learning Guide
WordPerfect 6 for DOS: The Visual Learning Guide
1-2-3 for Windows: The Visual Learning Guide
WordPerfect 6 for Windows: The Visual Learning Guide
Word for Windows 6: The Visual Learning Guide
Quicken 4 for Windows: The Visual Learning Guide

How to Order:

Quantity discounts are available from the publisher, Prima Publishing, P.O. Box 1260BK, Rocklin, CA 95677; FAX (916) 632-4405. On your letterhead include information concerning the intended use of the books and the number of books you wish to purchase.

Excel 5 for Windows
The Visual Learning Guide

Grace Joely Beatty, Ph.D.

David C. Gardner, Ph.D.

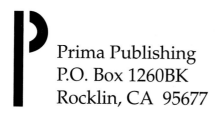

Prima Publishing
P.O. Box 1260BK
Rocklin, CA 95677

Library of Congress Catalog Card Number: 93-86727
ISBN: 1-55958-392-4

Executive Editor: Roger Stewart
Managing Editor: Neweleen A. Trebnik
Project Manager: Becky Freeman
Production and Layout: Marian Hartsough Associates
Interior Design: Grace Joely Beatty, S. Linda Beatty, David C. Gardner,
    Laurie Stewart, and Kim Bartusch
Technical Editing: Linda Miles
Cover Design: Page Design, Inc.
Color Separations: Ocean Quigley
Index: Katherine Stimson

Prima Publishing
Rocklin, CA 95677-1260

94 95 96 97 RRD 10 9 8 7 6 5 4 3

Printed in the United States of America

Acknowledgments

We are deeply indebted to reviewers around the country who gave generously of their time to test every step in the manuscript. David Coburn, Ray Holder, Jeannie Jones, and David Sauer cannot be thanked enough!

Carolyn Holder, Anne-Barbara Norris, and Linda Beatty are our in-house production team, reviewers, proofreaders, screen capturers, and friends. We could not possibly do what we do without them. They, along with Margaret Short, keep us functioning.

We are personally and professionally delighted to work with everyone at Prima Publishing, especially Roger Stewart, executive editor; Neweleen Trebnik, managing editor; Becky Freeman, project manager; Debbie Parisi, publicity coordinator; and Kim Bartusch, production coordinator.

Linda Miles, technical editor; Ocean Quigley, color separator; Marian Hartsough and Barbara Lewis, interior layout; and Paul Page, cover design, contributed immensely to the final product.

Bill Gladstone and Matt Wagner, of Waterside Productions, created the idea for this series. Their faith in us has never wavered.

Joseph and Shirley Beatty made this series possible. We can never repay them.

Asher Schapiro has always been there when we needed him.

Paula Gardner Capaldo and David Capaldo have been terrific. Thanks, Joshua and Jessica, for being such wonderful kids! Our project humorist, Mike Bumgardner, always came through when we needed a boost!

We could not have met the deadlines without the technical support of Ray Holder, our electrical genius, Fred Harper of Blue Line Communications, Inc., our computer genius, and Mark Hopwood of the Microsoft technical support staff. Thank you all!

Contents at a Glance

Customize Your Learning

Prima Visual Learning Guides are not like any other computer books you have ever seen. They are based on our years in the classroom, our corporate consulting, and our research at Boston University on the best ways to teach technical information to nontechnical learners. Most important, this series is based on the feedback of a panel of reviewers from across the country who range in computer knowledge from "panicked at the thought" to very sophisticated.

This is not an everything-you've-ever-wanted-to-know-about-Excel 5-but-didn't-know-enough-to-ask book. It is designed to give you the information you need to perform basic (and some not-so-basic) functions with confidence and skill. It is a book that our reviewers claim makes it "really easy" for anyone to learn Excel 5 quickly.

Each chapter is illustrated with full-color screen shots to guide you through every task. The combination of screens, step-by-step instructions, and pointers makes it impossible for you to get lost or confused as you follow along on your own computer. You can either work through from the beginning to the end or skip around to master skills you need. If you have a specific goal you want to accomplish now, choose it from the following list.

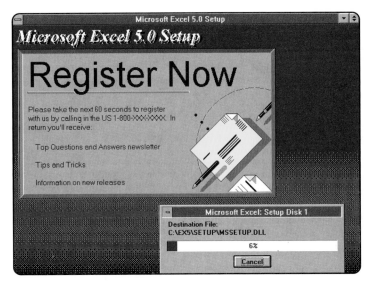

SELECT YOUR GOALS

From the list below, select your personal goals so that you can start using Excel 5 immediately.

❖ I would like help installing Excel 5.

Go to Appendix A.

❖ I'm new to Excel 5 and I want to learn how to set up a basic worksheet.

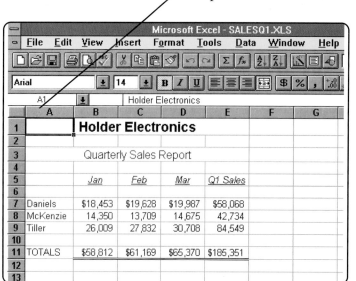

Turn to Part I to create a basic worksheet. Go on to Part II to add style to your worksheet.

You can learn how to write formulas in Chapter 13, "Writing Formulas."

❖ I want to learn how to work with multiple worksheets.

Turn to Part III. In this same part, you can also learn how to link worksheets together so that they share common information.

❖ I want to make a chart to illustrate the information on my worksheet.

Turn to Part IV. If you have not developed a worksheet from which to make a chart, go to Part I first.

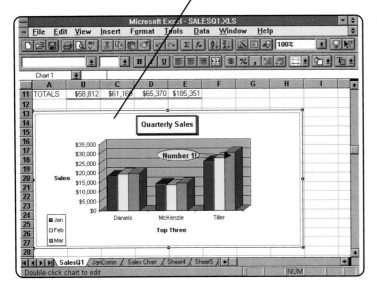

❖ I want to learn about Dynamic Data Exchange and the linking feature of Excel 5.

Go to Chapter 24.

Part I: Creating a Basic Worksheet

Setting Up a New Worksheet

The latest version of Excel makes it especially easy to create a worksheet, format and manipulate data, and take advantage of new features. In this chapter, you will do the following:

❖ Create a basic worksheet

❖ Complete a series

❖ Sort a column alphabetically

If you haven't installed Excel yet, turn to the Appendix, "Installing Excel 5."

OPENING EXCEL

1. **Type win** at the **c:\>** (C prompt) on your screen to boot up Windows if it is not already on your screen. Because Windows provides for tremendous customization, you will probably have different group icons than you see in this example.

Depending on how Excel was installed on your computer, there may be a separate group icon for Microsoft Office or Excel may have been moved to another group window.

If the Microsoft Office Group is already open, go to step 3 in this section.

2. **Click twice quickly** on the **group icon** that contains Excel. It will open up to a window. If you are new to windows, it may take a little time to get the right rhythm on the double-click. Don't worry if the icon jumps around a little when you click on it.

3. **Click twice** on the **Excel icon**. You will see an hourglass and then the copyright information for Excel. Then the opening screen for Excel will appear.

MAXIMIZING THE WORKSHEET

When you open (boot up) Excel for the first time, your screen may look like the example to the left. Notice that the worksheet does not fill the whole screen. You can change this very easily.

1. **Click** on the **Maximize button (▲)** on the right side of the Book 1 title bar. The worksheet will fill your screen.

THE EXCEL WORKBOOK

Notice "Book1" in the title bar. The Excel workbook is the equivalent of a three-ring binder that holds multiple sheets and chart sheets.

Notice the bar at the bottom of the workbook. You can have up to 255 sheets in a workbook. In Chapter 11, "Adding Worksheets to a Book," you will put a name on the tab to identify the worksheet.

This is a close-up view of a portion of the screen. You will see both close-up views and full-screen views in this book.

A worksheet is made up of *columns* and *rows*. The intersection of a column and a row forms a block, or *cell*. The *border* around the first cell on the worksheet tells you that this is the *active* cell. This is the cell that will be affected by the next entry or command.

Each cell has a unique *address*, or *reference*. The cell reference of the active cell shows in the Name box. The cell reference is A1 because the active cell is located in column A, row 1.

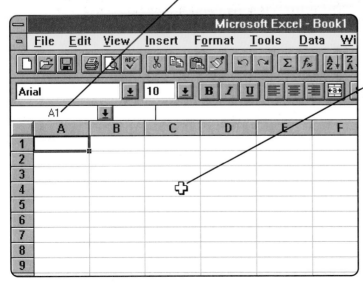

Notice, the mouse pointer has a plus-sign shape when it is in the worksheet area. The pointer changes shape depending on its location and the action you are performing.

ENTERING A WORKSHEET TITLE

When you create a worksheet, it is a good idea to enter a title. After the worksheet is printed, the worksheet title enables you (and others) to know the subject of the worksheet.

1. **Click** on cell **A1** if it does not already have a border around it. (On your screen, it will be blank.)

2. **Type** the word **Sales**. The letters will appear in the cell. They will also appear in the *contents box*, which displays characters as you type. If you make a typing error, just press the Backspace key and retype.

When you begin to type, notice than a red X (the *Cancel button*) and a green ✔ (the *Confirm button*) appear to the left of the contents box.

3 **Click** on ✔ to confirm that you want to enter "Sales" into A1. The Cancel and Confirm buttons will disappear after you confirm the entry.

ENTERING COLUMN HEADINGS

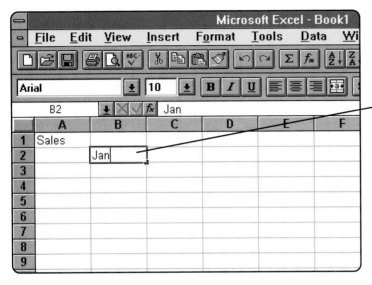

In this section, you will enter the abbreviation for January as the heading for column B.

1. **Click** on **B2**. On your screen, it will be blank.

2. **Type Jan**.

3. **Click** on the ✔ to confirm the entry.

USING THE AUTOFILL FEATURE TO COMPLETE A SERIES

After you have typed the first name in a common series (such as months in the year or days in the week), you can use the AutoFill feature to complete the series.

1. **Move** the mouse pointer **to the square** in the lower right corner of the cell. This square is called the *fill handle*. The pointer will change to a black plus sign. You may have to fiddle with the pointer to get it to change shape.

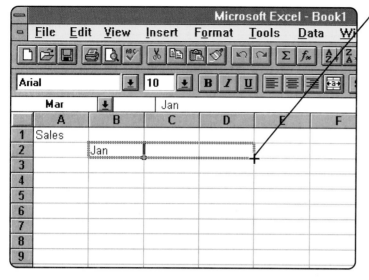

2. Press and hold the mouse button as you **drag** the fill handle **across columns C and D**. The border of the cell will expand as you drag.

3. Release the button. The AutoFill feature will automatically complete the series for you, as you can see in the next example.

If you want to include six months in the series, simply drag the fill handle across columns E, F, and G. Notice that February and March appeared as abbreviations. If you had typed "January," the succeeding months also would have been spelled out in full.

If you mistakenly fill in more cells in the series than you want, you can erase them. While the cells are highlighted, drag the fill handle backward to erase the unwanted names.

You can also drag the fill handle down the worksheet to create a series in a column format. It's an amazing feature!

ENTERING ROW HEADINGS

1. **Click** on **A3**. On your screen, the cell will be blank.

2. **Type** the name **Tiler**.

3. **Press Enter**. Tiler will be entered into the cell and the border will move to A4.

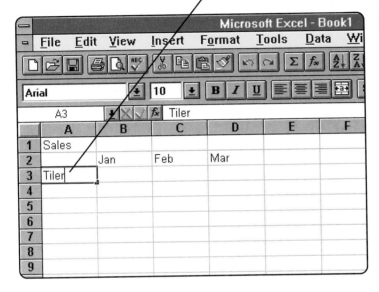

4. **Type** the name **Mackenzie**.

5. **Press Enter**. Notice that the name extends slightly into the next column and covers up the dividing line between columns. It's okay. You'll fix it after all the names are typed.

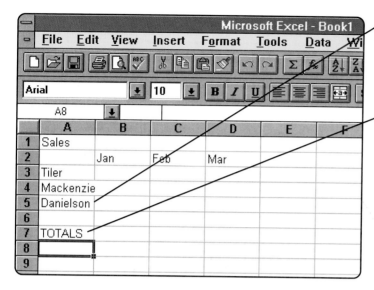

6. Type the name
Danielson.

7. Press Enter twice.

8. Type TOTALS in A7.

11. Press Enter.

Your worksheet will look
like the example to the left.

CHANGING THE COLUMN WIDTH

In this section, you will change the width of column A to accommodate the long name. You'll love the ease with which this happens.

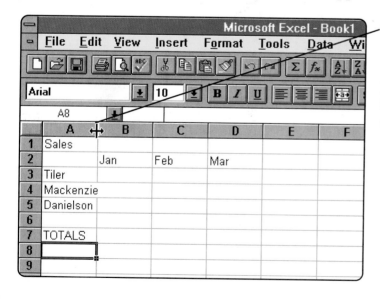

1. Place the mouse pointer on the **line between columns A** and **B**. The pointer will change to the shape you see in this example.

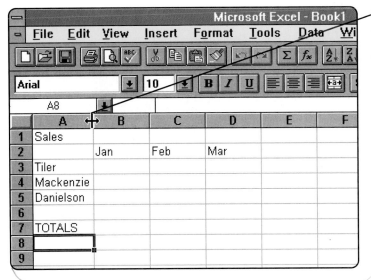

2. Click twice. The column will be expanded to a "best fit" width that takes into account the longest entry in the column. (Don't you love it?!) If nothing happens, try a faster speed on the double-clicks.

SORTING DATA ALPHABETICALLY

The capability to sort data after it has been entered in the worksheet is a helpful feature of Excel. In this section, you will sort the names in column A alphabetically.

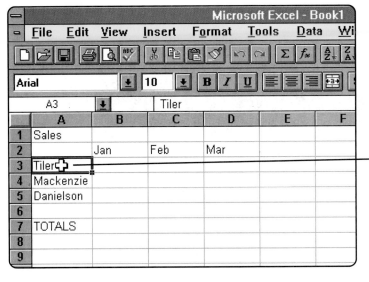

1. Click on **A3** and leave the pointer in the middle of the cell. Make sure that the pointer looks like a white plus sign.

2. **Press and hold** the mouse button and **drag** the pointer down to **A5**.

Notice the cell reference area indicates that you have highlighted three rows in one column (3Rx1C). This is called a *range* because the cells are adjacent to, or next to, each other.

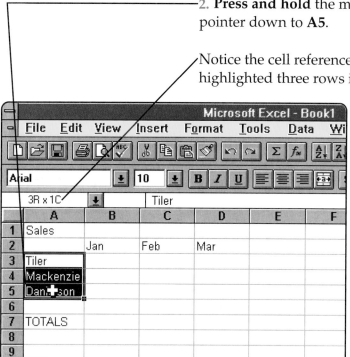

3. **Release** the mouse button when you have highlighted the range A3 through A5.

Notice that the range is highlighted in black except for the first cell, which remains white to tell you that this is the active cell.

4. **Click** on the **Sort Ascending button** (A to Z) in the toolbar. The names will be sorted alphabetically.

USING TOOLTIPS

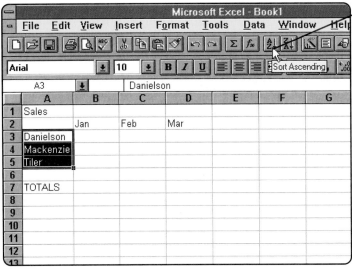

You may have noticed in the previous section that when you placed your pointer in the lower right corner of the Sort button, a yellow box describing the button's function appeared. You can use the Tooltips feature for any button at the top of the screen to find out what the button does. Try it!

ENTERING NUMBERS

1. **Click** on **B3**. On your screen, the cell will be empty.

2. **Type** the number **18453**.

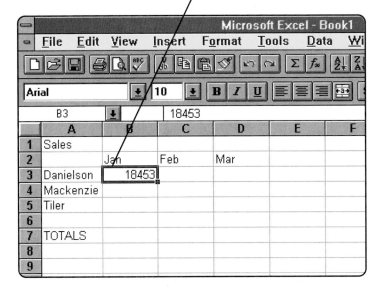

3. **Press** ↓ (the down-arrow key on your keyboard) to enter the number into B3 and automatically move the selection border to B4. Using the arrow keys on your keyboard is another way to enter data and move around the worksheet. (If you are using the arrows on the numeric keyboard, make sure that the Num Lock key is turned off.)

4. **Enter** the **numbers** shown on the screen to the left in the appropriate cells on your worksheet.

Remember that there are several ways to confirm that you want to enter data into the worksheet:

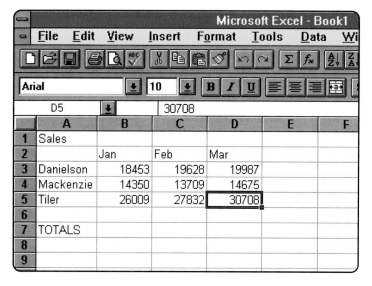

❖ Click on ✔.

❖ Press Enter. This will enter the data into the cell and move the border to the next cell down.

❖ Press an arrow key on your keyboard to enter the data and move the selection border to the next cell in the direction of the arrow.

Notice that numbers are automatically aligned on the right in a cell. Text is aligned on the left.

This worksheet will be used throughout the rest of this book. In Chapter 3, "Editing Your Worksheet," you will make corrections to this worksheet.

Naming and Saving a Workbook

Because Excel is a Windows-based program, it uses standard windows commands to name and save files. In this chapter, you will do the following:

❖ Name a workbook using the Save As command
❖ Save a workbook

NAMING A WORKBOOK

Use the Save As command to name a workbook. You can have up to eight characters in the name. Excel will automatically add the .XLS extension to identify this as a worksheet file.

1. **Click** on **File** in the menu bar. A pull-down menu will appear.

2. **Click** on **Save As**. The Save As dialog box will appear. It may appear in a different spot on your screen than what you see in the next example.

Because Book1 in the File Name text box is already highlighted, you can simply begin to type the new filename.

3. **Type salesq1**. (Filenames can have up to eight characters and no spaces). It will replace the highlighted text.

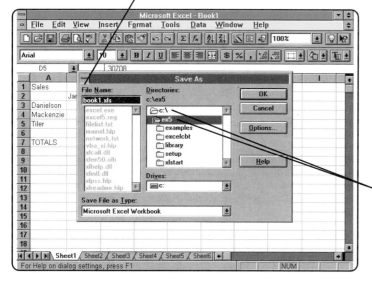

It doesn't matter whether you type the filename in capital or small letters. The filename will appear in capital letters on the titlebar. Excel will automatically add the .XLS extension to identify it as a worksheet.

The open file folders next to "c:\" and "ex5" indicate that the file will be saved on the C drive in the ex5 (Excel 5) directory. If you chose a directory other than ex5 when you installed Excel, the second open folder will be beside that directory.

4. **Click** on **OK**. The Summary Info dialog box will appear.

You do not have to enter anything in the Summary Info dialog box. However, it's useful for future reference to enter information that will help identify a file and its purpose.

The screen to your left is an example of the kind of information you might want to enter. You can enter the data if you want. Press the Tab key to move from one text box to another.

5. Click on **OK**. The Summary Info dialog box will close. Your file is then saved.

SAVING A FILE

Develop the habit of saving your file while you work on it. Save often. This habit will spare you much grief and aggravation in the event of a power failure or equipment problem.

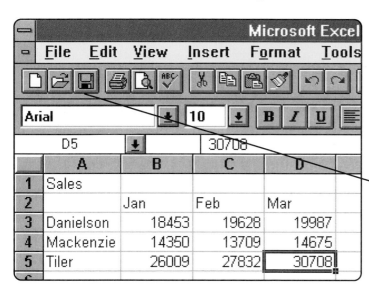

With the Save File button, you can save with a click of your mouse.

1. Click on the **Save File button** in the toolbar. An hourglass will appear briefly as Excel saves your workbook. Do this step often.

Editing Your Worksheet

Editing is straightforward in Excel because of one of Excel's newest features, in-cell editing, which allows you to edit the contents of a cell directly in the cell. Using the mouse gives you a great deal of control in the editing process. You can change the contents of a cell, change individual letters or numbers in a cell, clear a cell completely, or even undo your edit if you change your mind. In this chapter, you will do the following:

❖ Make edits to the worksheet you created in Chapter 1 so that you can use the worksheet throughout the rest of this book

❖ Cancel an edit

❖ Use Undo

ADDING DATA

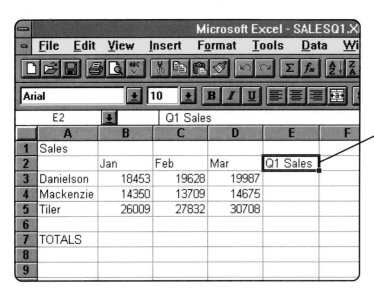

You can add data at any time to a worksheet. In this section, you will add the heading "Q1 Sales" to Column E.

1. **Click** on **E2**. On your screen, it will be blank.

2. **Type Q1 Sales** and **press Enter**.

INSERTING A CHARACTER INTO A CELL

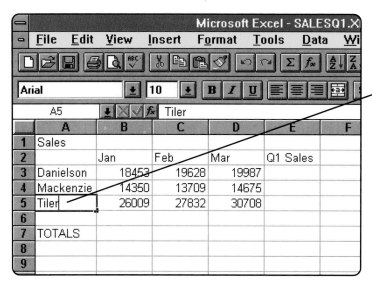

In this section, you will change the name "Tiler" to "Tiller" with in-cell editing.

1. **Click twice** on **Tiler** in **A5**. Your cursor will begin flashing in the cell and Tiler will appear in the contents box.

2. **Press** the ← **key** on your keyboard twice to place the flashing bar between the letters *l* and *e*.

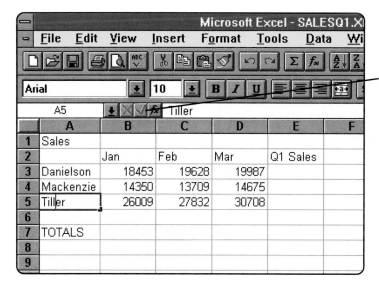

3. **Type** the letter l. It will be added to the name.

4. **Click** on ✔ or press Enter to enter the change in the cell.

DELETING A CHARACTER FROM A CELL

In this section, you will change the name "Mackenzie" to "McKenzie."

Deleting to the Right

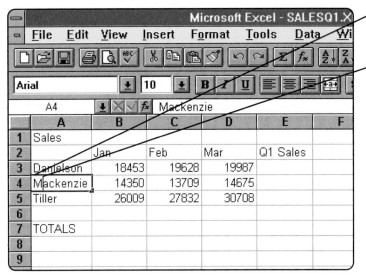

1. **Click twice** on Mackenzie in **A4**.

2. **Place** the mouse pointer between the letters *M* and *a*. The pointer will change to an I-beam.

3. **Click** to set the cursor in place. It will change to a flashing bar.

4. **Press** the **Delete key** to delete the letter *a*.

Deleting to the Left

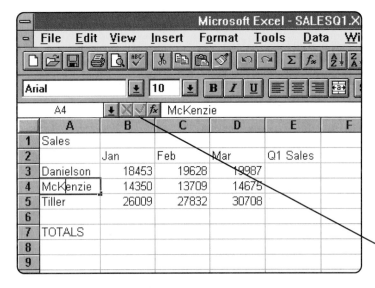

1. **Press** the → **key twice** to move the flashing bar to the right of the letter *k*.

2. **Press** the **Backspace key** to delete the *k*.

3. **Type** a capital **K** to make the name McKenzie.

4. **Click** on ✔ or press Enter.

DELETING MORE THAN ONE CHARACTER

You can edit the contents of a cell in the contents box. In this section, you will change the name "Danielson" to "Daniels."

1. Click *once* on Danielson in **A3**.

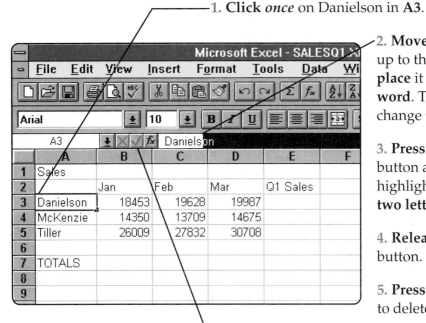

2. Move the mouse pointer up to the contents box and **place** it at the **end** of the **word**. The pointer will change to an I-beam.

3. Press and hold the mouse button as you **drag** the highlight bar over the **last two letters** in the name.

4. Release the mouse button.

5. Press the **Backspace key** to delete the letters.

6. Click on ✔ or press Enter to confirm the change.

CANCELING AN EDIT

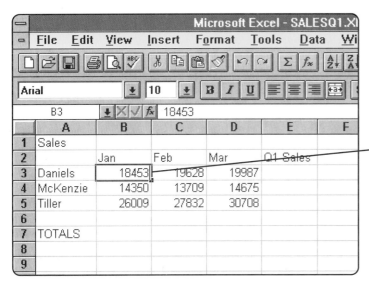

If you're like the rest of us, you occasionally make a change you didn't intend to make. If you catch the mistake before you confirm the change, you can undo it.

1. **Click twice** on **B3**.

2. **Place** the **cursor** at the **beginning** of the number. The cursor will change to an I-beam.

3. **Click** the mouse button **twice**. The contents of the cell will be highlighted.

4. **Type** the number **20000**. It will replace the highlighted number. (Do *not* press Enter.)

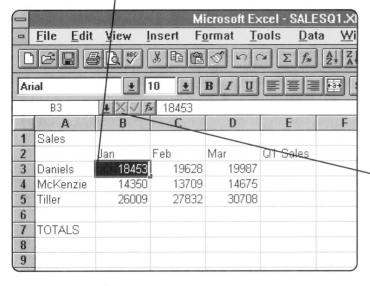

At this point, you discover that you should not have changed the number. Because you are still in the cell and you have not pressed Enter, you can simply cancel the change.

5. **Click** on × (the Cancel button) in the edit bar to undo the change. The original number, 18453, will appear again.

USING UNDO

If you actually enter a change and then decide that you don't want it, you can undo the change with the Undo button as long as you use it before you perform any other function.

In this section, you will clear the contents of a cell and then undo the change.

1. **Click** once on TOTALS in **A7**.

2. **Press** the **Delete key**. The contents of the cell will be cleared.

3. **Click** on **B7**.

4. **Click** on the **Undo button** in the toolbar. The contents of A7 will be restored and the selection border will move back to A7. Even though you moved to a new cell, you did not perform an actual function, such as entering data or using a menu bar command. Therefore, you can use the Undo button.

A general rule of thumb is that you can use the ✕ (Cancel button) when it is visible. If it is not visible, use the Undo button.

Totaling
Columns and Rows

This is the fun part! Excel 5 has a wonderful icon that contains a built-in formula to sum columns and rows. You can total individual columns and rows and then use features such as AutoFill and Fill Right to copy the formula to other columns and rows. Or, you can highlight a range of cells and use the AutoSum button to total all columns and rows with one command. In this chapter, you will do the following:

❖ Use the AutoSum button to sum columns and rows

USING THE AUTOSUM BUTTON

Although you can write a formula to total a column or row, clicking on the AutoSum button creates the formula for you automatically. (You will learn how to write formulas in Chapter 13, "Writing Formulas and Using the Subtotal Feature.")

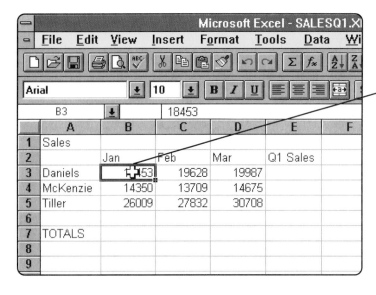

Highlighting a Range

1. **Click** on **B3.** Leave the pointer in the cell.

2. **Press and hold** the mouse button and **drag** the pointer down to **E7**. The range B3 to E7 will be highlighted.

3. **Click** on the **AutoSum button** in the toolbar. (Σ is the Greek symbol for *sum*.) Sums will appear in column E and row 7.

Your screen will look like this example.

4. **Click** on the **Save button** in the toolbar to save your work.

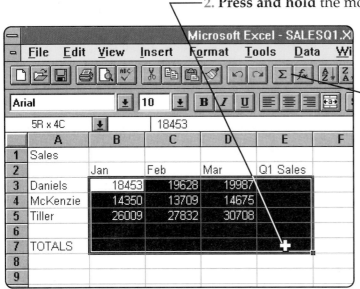

Using Page Setup, Print Preview and Printing a File

When you print a file in Excel, you can customize the printed page in a number of ways. For example, you can add identifying information to a file with headers and footers. You can remove the gridlines you see on your screen and center the worksheet horizontally and vertically on the page. You can even preview a file to see what it will look like before it prints. In this chapter, you will do the following:

❖ Print a worksheet
❖ Use the Page Setup options
❖ Add a header to a file
❖ Use the Print Preview feature

USING THE PRINT BUTTON

1. **Click** on the **Print button** in the toolbar. A Printing message box will appear.

	A	B	C	D	E	F
1	Sales					
2		Jan	Feb	Mar	Q1 Sales	
3	Daniels	18453	19628	19987	58068	
4	McKenzie	14350	13709	14675	42734	
5	Tiller	26009	27832	30708	84549	
6						
7	TOTALS	58812	61169	65370	185351	
8						
9						

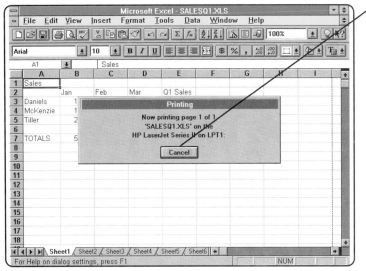

Notice that you can click on Cancel in the message box if you want to cancel the print command. Because the file is short, the message box will appear only briefly. It will be on the screen for a longer time for a longer file.

USING PAGE SETUP OPTIONS

You can customize many features of printing in Excel by using Page Setup options. The settings you make in the Page Setup dialog box affect only this particular worksheet. If you have multiple worksheets in a file (as you will in Part III), you have to do Page Setup options for each worksheet.

Opening the Page Setup Dialog Box

1. **Click** on **File** in the menu bar. A pull-down list will appear.

2. **Click** on **Page Setup**. The Page Setup dialog box will appear.

The Page Setup dialog box has four sections, or tabs: Page, Margins, Header/Footer, and Sheet. First you will go to the Margins section.

Centering the Worksheet on the Printed Page

You can enter your worksheet both horizontally and vertically on the printed page. This will have no effect on how the worksheet appears on the screen. In this example, you will center the worksheet horizontally.

1. **Click** on the **Margins Tab** to go to the Margins options.

2. **Click** on **Horizontally** to insert an X in the box. When the file prints, the worksheet will be centered across the page.

Changing Margins

The worksheet is set up with standard (default) margins of 1 inch at the top and bottom and .75 inch on the left and right. In this example, you will change the top margin.

1. **Click twice** in the **Top Margin box**. The box will be highlighted.

Notice that a bold line appears in the Preview box in the top margin position, indicating that the top margin is currently selected.

2. **Type 2**. It will replace the highlighted text.

Adding a Header

A *header* is a line of type added to the top of the printed page. It usually contains identifying data, such as the filename or the date, but it can be any text you want. A header can be aligned with the left margin, centered, or aligned with the right margin.

1. **Click** on the **Header/ Footer Tab** to move to the Header/Footer options.

2. Click on **Custom Header**. The Header dialog box will appear.

3. Click twice on the **Center Section** position to highlight the &[Tab]. (This code prints the name you give to Sheet1 in the header. You will learn how to name Sheet1 in the section entitled "Naming Worksheets," in Chapter 11.

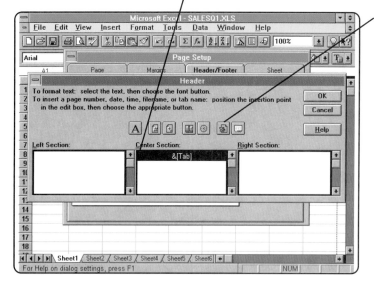

4. Click on the **filename button**. It will replace the highlighted text.

5. Press the **Enter key** to add a second line in the Center Section box.

6. **Click** on the **date button**. The code for date will be inserted in the box.

The other icons in this dialog box insert the following information:

 Brings up the font dialog box

Page number

Number of pages in a document

Time of printing

Sheet name

7. **Click** on **OK**. The Header/Footer options will reappear.

Deleting a Footer

Your worksheet is set up to print "Page 1" at the bottom of the page. In this example, you will delete the page number.

1. **Click** on the **Custom Footer button**. The Footer dialog box will appear.

2. **Click** to the **left** of **Page &[Page]**. This code prints the word "Page" and then the page number.)

3. **Press and hold** the mouse button and **drag** the cursor across **Page &[Page]**. The text will be highlighted.

4. **Press** the **Delete key** on your keyboard. The text will be deleted.

5. **Click** on **OK**. The Header/Footer options will reappear.

Removing Gridlines From the Printing Page

Your page will print with the same gridlines you see on your screen unless you remove them.

1. **Click** on the **Sheet Tab**. The Sheet options will appear.

2. **Click** on **Gridlines** to *remove* the ✕ from the box. If you leave the ✕ in the box, the worksheet will print with gridlines on it. Removing the gridlines from the printed page will not affect the gridlines on your screen.

Increasing the Size of the Worksheet on the Printed Page

You can significantly enlarge the size of the worksheet on the printed page. This capacity is especially helpful if you plan to use the page in a presentation.

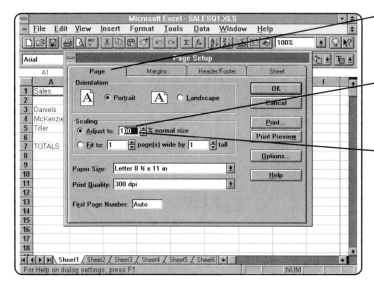

1. **Click** on the **Page Tab**. The Page options will appear.

2. **Click** to the **right** of **"100"** in the Adjust to box to set the cursor.

3. **Press and hold** the mouse button and **drag** the cursor backward **over** the **00** in 100. The 0s will be highlighted.

4. **Release** the mouse button.

5. Type 50 to make the enlargement factor 150%. You can use such a big enlargement factor because SALESQ1 doesn't have a great deal of data in it. Experiment with different sizes. If you want a smaller print size than normal, type a number less than 100. (This size affects the printout only. To change the size of the type on your printout *and* on the screen, see the section "Increasing Type Size," in Chapter 9.

6. Click on **OK**. The SALESQ1 worksheet will appear.

PREVIEWING THE PAGE

1. Click on the **Print Preview button** in the toolbar. The Print Preview dialog box will appear.

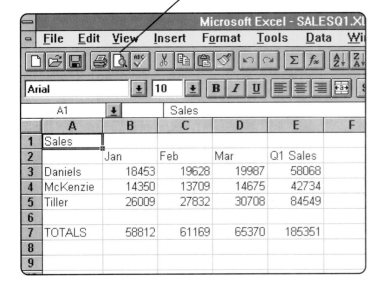

Using the Zoom Feature

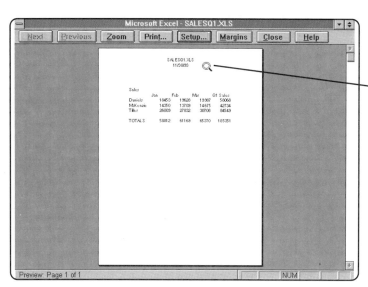

In the Preview screen, the pointer looks like a magnifying glass.

1. **Place** the **magnifying glass** over the worksheet **area** you want to see more closely.

2. **Click** the **mouse button**. The area you selected will be enlarged.

3. **Click** the **mouse button** again to return to the full-page view.

Changing the Margins Through the Preview Screen

Notice that the header appears at the top of the page and is not affected by the position of the top margin. In the Print Preview screen, you can change margins with your mouse. In this section, you will change the top margin back to 1 inch.

1. **Click** on the **Margins button** if the margin lines are not showing.

2. **Place** the mouse pointer on the **handle** (the black square) on the **top margin line**. The pointer will change to the shape you see in this example.

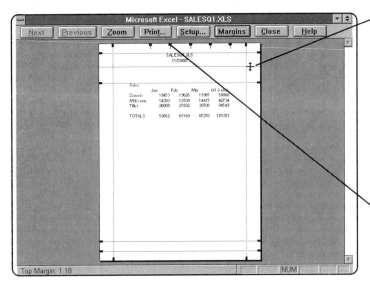

3. Press and hold the mouse button as you **drag** the line up so that it is approximately 1 inch from the top of the page.

4. Release the mouse button when the line is positioned where you want it.

You can change the column width by dragging the column handles using the same method as above.

PRINTING THROUGH THE PRINT PREVIEW SCREEN

1. Click on **Print** to print the document. The Print dialog box will appear. (**Or click** on **Close** to close the Preview screen without printing.)

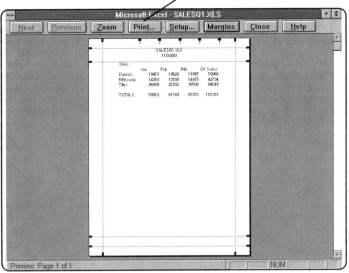

2. Click on **Selected Sheet(s)** to put a dot in the circle if one is not already there. This step will print only the worksheet on which you are currently working.

3. Click on **OK**. A Printing message box will appear and your worksheet will print.

You can also print by clicking on File in the menu bar and then on Print in the pull-down menu. The Print dialog box will appear, as shown above.

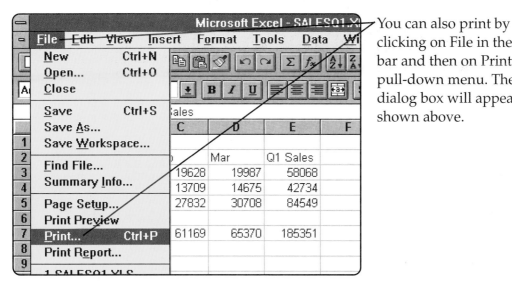

Closing A Workbook and Exiting Excel

In Windows-based programs, you can often accomplish the same task in several different ways. Excel 5 is no exception. In this chapter you will do the following:

❖ Learn a quick way to close a workbook

❖ Learn a quick way to exit Excel

CLOSING A WORKBOOK

When you close a workbook, you do not exit Excel. If no other workbooks are open, the blank Excel Window will appear.

1. **Click twice** on the **Control menu box** ⊟ on the left side of the menu bar. A Microsoft Excel dialog box will appear. Be careful not to click on the top Control menu box on the Excel title bar. This will close Excel.

2. **Click** on **Yes**.

If you click on No, any changes you made to the file since the last time you saved will be lost. If you click on Cancel, the dialog box will disappear and you will be returned to the worksheet.

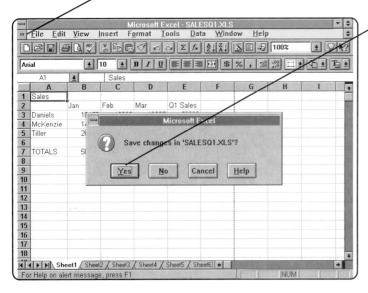

EXITING EXCEL

If you have been following along with the steps in this chapter, you closed the SALESQ1 workbook and the blank Excel window is on your screen. If you did not close the workbook on your screen, this exit procedure will work anyway.

1. **Click twice** on the **Control menu box** (⊟) on the left side of the Excel title bar. If you saved before doing this, Excel will close.

If you forgot to save, Excel will rescue you and ask whether you want to save.

2. **Click** on **Yes** to save and exit Excel.

OPENING EXCEL

If you want to continue to Chapter 7, "Opening a Saved Workbook," reopen Excel.

1. **Click twice** on the **Microsoft Excel icon**. The Excel opening screen will appear.

Program Manager

Part II: Adding Style to Your Worksheet

Opening a Saved Workbook

Excel makes opening a saved workbook file as easy as clicking your mouse. In this chapter, you will do the following:

❖ Open the SALESQ1.XLS file by using the File pull-down menu

❖ Open the SALESQ1.XLS file by using the Open File button

OPENING A SAVED WORKBOOK

Excel has a special feature in the file pull-down menu that makes opening a saved workbook file especially easy.

Method #1

1. **Click** on **File** in the menu bar. A pull-down menu will appear.

The File pull-down menu lists the four most recent files that were opened. If others have used Excel before you, there may be up to four filenames on the list. As you create workbooks, the list will change.

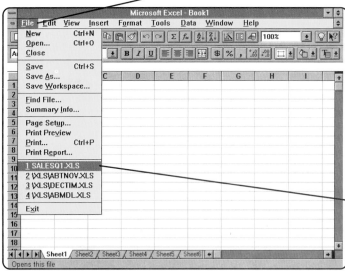

2. **Click** on **SALESQ1.XLS**. The workbook will appear.

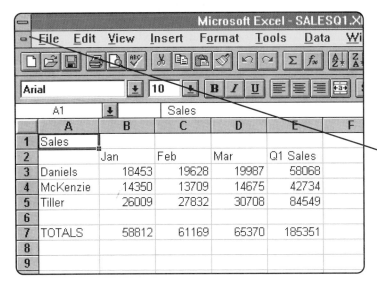

If you want to try method #2, you need to close SALESQ1.XLS first. Because you have made no changes to SALESQ1.XLS, there is no need to save.

3. **Click twice** on the **Control menu box** (⊟) on the left side of the menu bar. The worksheet will close.

Method #2

Excel has a button on the toolbar for locating and opening a workbook file.

1. **Click** on the **Open File button** on the toolbar. The Open dialog box will appear.

2. Click twice on **salesq1.xls**. The SALESQ1.XLS workbook will open.

Adding and Deleting Rows

As part of the process of adding and deleting rows, you will use an Excel feature called a *shortcut menu*. If you think that clicking on the menu bar and getting a pull-down menu is easy, just wait until you use a shortcut menu! In this chapter, you will do the following;

❖ Add rows

❖ Delete a row

❖ Using a shortcut menu

ADDING ROWS

Suppose that you want the company name on the SALESQ1.XLS worksheet for a presentation tomorrow. In this section, you will add three rows at the beginning of the SALESQ1.XLS worksheet so that you can add the company name. You will also add some other blank rows within the worksheet.

Using a Shortcut Menu

1. **Click** on the **row 1 button**. The entire row will be highlighted. Leave the mouse pointer on the row.

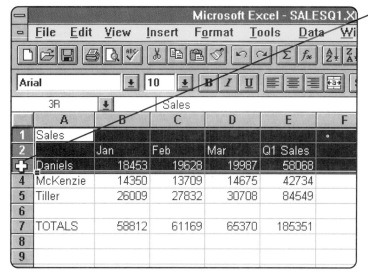

2. Press and hold the mouse button and **drag** the highlight bar down to **row 3**. *Leave the mouse pointer in the highlighted area.* When you are getting ready to use a shortcut menu, it's important that you leave the mouse pointer in the highlighted area or else the next step won't work.

3. Click on the **right** mouse button. A shortcut menu will appear.

4. Click on **Insert**. Three rows will be inserted at the top of the worksheet. All following rows will be renumbered. Excel knew to insert rows because you used the row buttons to select the number of rows to be added.

5. **Click** on the **row 5 button**. The entire row will be highlighted. Leave the pointer in the cell.

6. **Click** the **right** mouse button. A shortcut menu will appear.

7. **Click** on **Insert**. A row will be inserted at the cursor point. All following rows will be renumbered.

Using the Insert Menu

In this example, you will add a row above the names by using the Insert pull-down menu.

1. **Click** on Daniels in **A7**.

2. **Click** on **Insert** in the menu bar. A pull-down menu will appear.

3. **Click** on **Rows**. A row will be added to the worksheet.

DELETING A ROW

After looking at your worksheet, you decide that three rows at the top are too many. Don't worry. Deleting is easy.

1. **Click** on the **row 1 button**. This step will select the entire row. Leave the pointer in the row.

2. **Click** the **right** mouse button. A shortcut menu will appear.

3. **Click** on **Delete**. The highlighted row will be deleted and all following rows will be renumbered.

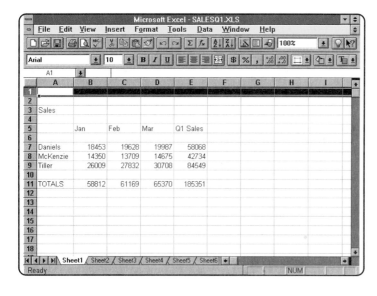

Your worksheet will look like this example.

ADDING A WORKSHEET HEADING

In this section, you will add the company name to the worksheet and change "Sales" to a more descriptive heading.

1. Click on **A1**. On your screen, the cell will be empty.

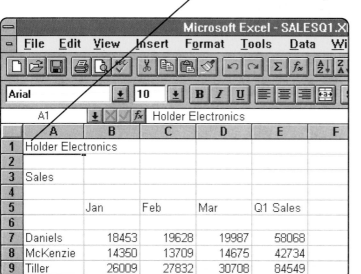

2. Type Holder Electronics. Don't be concerned that the name is too long for the cell. As long as the cell to the right is empty, the entry will expand into the next cell.

3. Press Enter to insert the name into A1. You will center the company name over the worksheet in the section "Centering Across Columns and Within Cells," in Chapter 9.

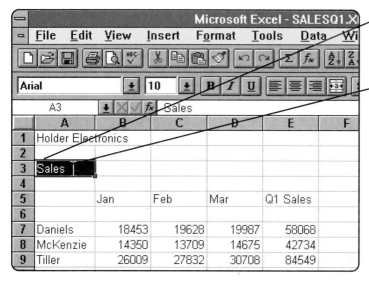

4. Click twice on sales in **A3** to activate the cell for in-cell editing.

5. With the I-beam in the cell, **click twice**. The contents of the cell will be highlighted.

6. Type the words **Quarterly Sales Report**. They will replace the highlighted text.

7. Press Enter to insert "Quarterly Sales Report" in A3.

8. **Click** on the **Save button** on the toolbar to save the changes in your worksheet.

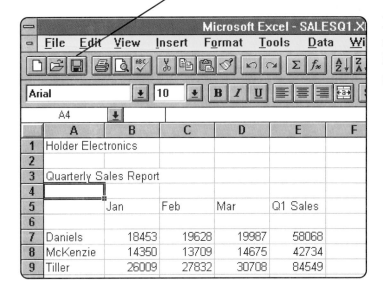

In the next chapter, you will dress up the worksheet with larger type boldface print, and other style changes.

Formatting the Worksheet

Excel has many buttons available right on the toolbar that will help improve the appearance of your worksheet. These buttons make formatting your worksheet a snap. In this chapter, you will do the following:

❖ Increase the font size

❖ Change the type style to bold

❖ Change the type style to italics

❖ Underline text

❖ Add a border to a cell

❖ Center across columns and within cells

INCREASING FONT SIZE

Notice that Excel is set up to print with an Arial font, or type style, in a 10-point size. In this section, you will learn how to increase font size.

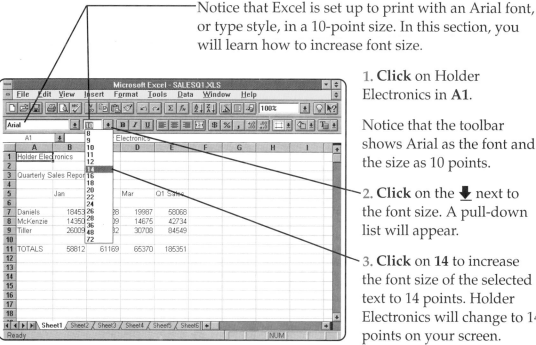

1. Click on Holder Electronics in **A1**.

Notice that the toolbar shows Arial as the font and the size as 10 points.

2. Click on the ⬇ next to the font size. A pull-down list will appear.

3. Click on **14** to increase the font size of the selected text to 14 points. Holder Electronics will change to 14 points on your screen.

4. Click on Quarterly Sales Report in **A3**.

5. Click on the ⬇ next to the font size. A pull-down list will appear.

6. Click on **12** to increase the font size of the selected text to 12 points. "Quarterly Sales Report" will change to 12 point-size on your screen.

A Note About Appearances

Even though "Quarterly Sales Report" appears to extend into cell B3, Excel considers it to be in cell A3. Therefore, when you click on A3, all three words show in the edit line. Try clicking on cell B3. Notice that nothing shows in the edit line because nothing was actually entered into cell B3. Interesting. . . .

Notice also when you click on B3 that the font size shown in the Font Size box is 10. The reason is that you applied the 12-point size to A3, not to B3.

ADDING AND REMOVING BOLDFACE FROM TYPE

In Excel, many buttons work like toggle switches. Click to turn the function on and then click again to turn it off. In this section, you will make text bold, then turn off the boldface, and then turn it on again. First select the cell you want to change.

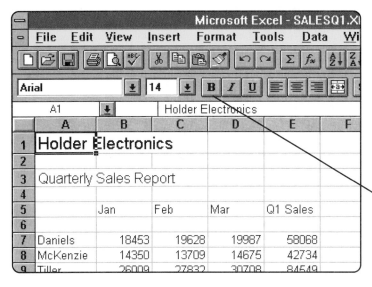

1. **Click** on Holder Electronics in **A1**.

2. **Click** on the **Bold button** on the toolbar (the large B). The text in A1 will be made bold.

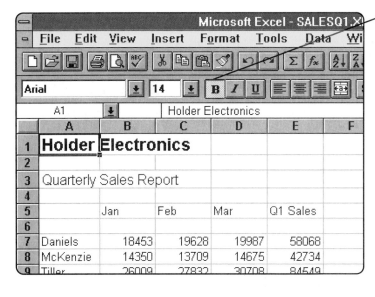

Notice that the Bold button now appears lighter and pressed in. This tells you that this feature is currently turned on for the cell.

3. While the cell is still selected, **click** on the **Bold button** again to make the type normal.

4. **Click** on the **Bold button** again to make the text boldface once more.

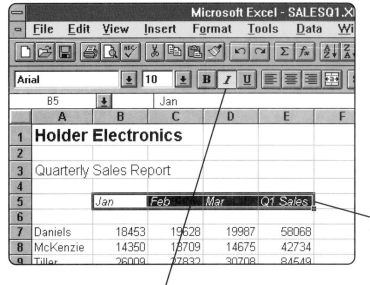

MAKING TEXT ITALIC

In this section, you will highlight a range of cells and, with one command, apply italics to the entire range.

1. **Click** on Jan in **B5**. Leave the pointer in the cell.

2. **Press and hold** the mouse button and **drag** the pointer over to Q1 Sales in **E5**. Then release the mouse button.

3. **Click** on the **Italics button** on the toolbar (the large, slanted I). The text in all the cells will be italicized.

UNDERLINING TEXT

If you have been following along with these examples, cells B5 through E5 are highlighted.

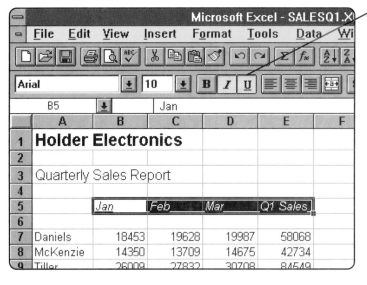

1. **Click** on the **Underline button** on the toolbar (the large, underlined U). The highlighted text from the previous section will be underlined.

2. **Click anywhere** on the worksheet to remove the highlighting so that you can see the italics and underlining in cells B5 through E5.

CREATING A DOUBLE UNDERLINE

In this section, you will put a double underline beneath the totals in row 11.

1. **Click** on **B11**. Leave the pointer in the cell.

2. **Press and hold** the mouse button and **drag** the pointer over to **E11**.

3. **Release** the mouse button when you have highlighted B11 through E11.

4. **Click** on the ⬇ to the right of the Borders button in the toolbar. The borders box will appear.

5. **Click** on the **double underline button**. The Borders box will disappear and B11 through E11 will be underlined.

6. **Click anywhere** on the worksheet to remove the highlighting so that you can see the double underline.

Notice that the double underline border is applied to the cell itself. This contrasts with the underline feature in the previous section, which applied to the *contents* of the cell.

CENTERING ACROSS COLUMNS

Text in a cell is normally aligned on the left. In this section, you will highlight rows 1 through 3 and apply the centering option to all of them at the same time.

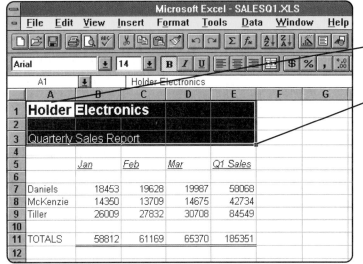

1. **Click** on **A1**. Leave the pointer in the cell.

2. **Press and hold** the mouse button and **drag** the pointer diagonally down to **E3**.

3. **Release** the mouse button when you have highlighted cells A1 through E3.

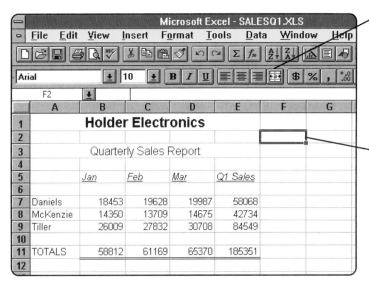

4. **Click** on the **Center Across Columns button** on the toolbar. The company name and worksheet title will be centered across the highlighted columns.

5. **Click anywhere** on the worksheet to remove the highlighting and see the centering.

CENTERING WITHIN CELLS

In this example, you will center the text in row 5 in each cell.

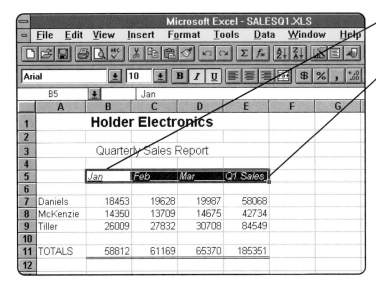

1. **Click** on **B5**. Leave the pointer in the cell.

2. **Press and hold** the mouse button and **drag** the pointer horizontally across to **E5**.

3. **Release** the mouse button when you have highlighted cells B1 through E5.

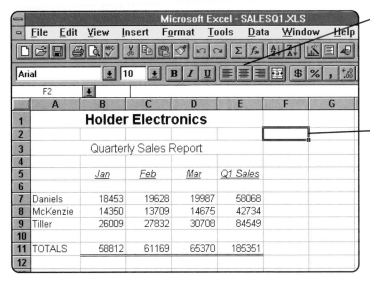

4. **Click** on the **Center button** on the toolbar. The column headers in the table will be centered in their respective cells.

5. **Click anywhere** on the worksheet to remove the highlighting and see the centering.

You will format the numbers on the worksheet in the next chapter.

Formatting Numbers and Working with Styles

The standard (or default) style for numbers is called the Normal number style. You can change this style and format numbers so that they appear with dollar signs, commas, decimals, or percentages. Numbers can be rounded off to a specific decimal place or whole number or made to appear with a minus sign or parentheses to indicate a negative number. You can format numbers to appear as dates or times, or in the specialized style called scientific notation. You can even save specific formatting as a style and then apply that style to another set of numbers. In this chapter, you will do the following:

❖ Format the numbers already in a worksheet

❖ Format non-adjacent cells with a single command

❖ Save a specific format as a style and apply that style to other numbers

❖ Remove and restore styles in a worksheet

INSERTING COMMAS IN NUMBERS

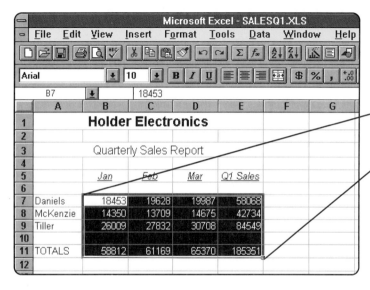

In this example, you will apply the comma style to the numbers on the worksheet.

1. Click on **B7**. Leave the pointer in the cell.

2. Press and hold the mouse button and **drag** the pointer diagonally down to **E11**. Then release the mouse button.

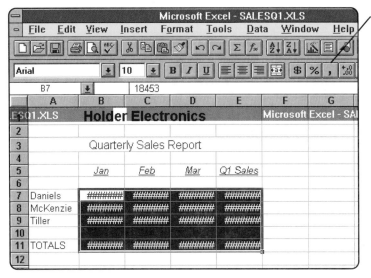

3. **Click** on the **Comma button** on the toolbar.

Notice that some (or all) of the numbers have changed to number signs (#). Don't panic. This simply means that the numbers are now too long for the cells because the comma style includes two decimal places. If you want the decimal places to show, you can change the cell width, as you did in the section entitled, "Changing the Column Width," in Chapter 1. In this example, you will remove the decimal places.

4. **Click twice** on the **Decrease Decimal button** on the toolbar. Each click will remove a zero.

ADDING DOLLAR SIGNS

In this section, you will use the Format menu rather than a toolbar button to add the Currency style to the first and last rows of numbers. If you use the Ctrl key, you can highlight non-adjacent rows (or columns or cells) and apply a command to all highlighted areas at one time.

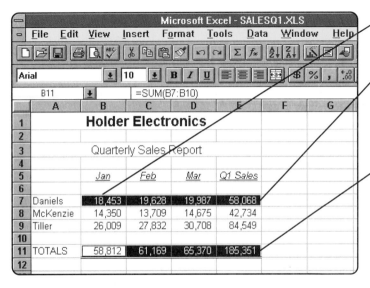

1. Click on **B7**. Leave the pointer in the cell.

2. Press and hold the mouse button and **drag** the pointer over to **E7**. Then **release** the mouse button.

3. Press and hold the **Ctrl key** and **repeat steps 1 and 2** to highlight cells B11:E11. (B11:E11 is another way to say B11 through E11.) Make sure to leave the mouse pointer in the highlighted area or the next step won't work.

4. Click the **right** mouse button. A shortcut menu will appear.

5. Click on **Format Cells**. The Format Cells dialog box will appear.

6. Click on **Currency** in the Category list.

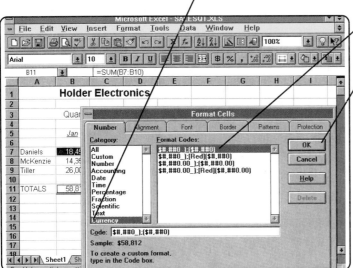

7. Click on **$#,##0_);(#,##0)** in the Format Codes list.

8. Click on **OK**.

Depending on the version of the Arial font you have, the number in E11 may still be too long for the cell. If so, use the mouse to increase the width of column E. Refer to "Changing Column Width" in Chapter 1 if you need help.

NAMING A STYLE

Number format, font, borders, and alignment are some of the elements that make up the *style* of a cell. If you use a certain style frequently, you can save it as a Named Style and then apply the Named Style to another cell or range. In this section, you will select cell B11 and name the style of the cell "totals."

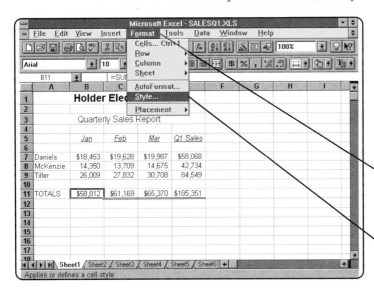

1. Click on **B11**.

2. Click on **Format** in the menu bar. A pull-down menu will appear.

3. Click on **Style**. The Style dialog box will appear.

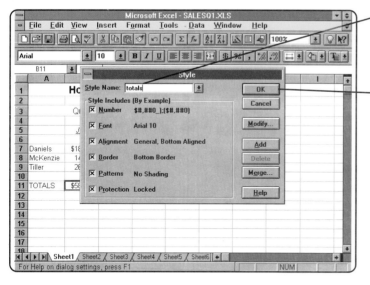

4. Type totals. It will replace the highlighted text in the style Name box.

5. Click on **OK**. The formatting in B11 is now saved as the style "totals."

REMOVING AND RESTORING FORMATS AND STYLES

If you decide that you don't like a particular format or style, you can remove it with the Undo command if you use it immediately after applying the style. There are, however, other ways to remove unwanted styles.

Clearing Formats

1. Click on **B11** and leave the pointer in the cell.

2. Press and hold the mouse button and **drag** the highlight bar across to **E11**.

3. Click on **Edit** in the menu bar. A pull-down menu will appear.

4. Click on **Clear**. A second menu will appear.

5. Click on **Formats**. The worksheet will reappear. The formatting styles you applied to the highlighted cells will be removed.

Applying a Named Style

First highlight the cell or range to which you want to apply a Named Style. If you have been following along with these examples, B11:E11 is already highlighted.

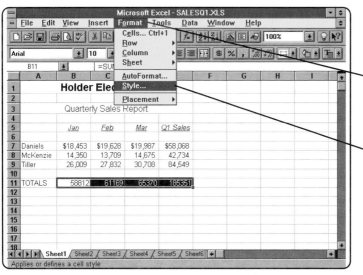

1. Click on **Format** in the menu bar. A pull-down menu will appear.

2. Click on **Style**. The Style dialog box will appear.

3. Click on the ⬇ to the right of the Style Name box. A drop-down list will appear.

4. Click on **"totals"**. The drop-down list will disappear and "totals" will be in the Style Name box.

5. Click on **OK**. The Style dialog box will disappear and the worksheet will appear with the "totals" style applied to the highlighted cells.

6. Click anywhere on the worksheet to remove the highlighting.

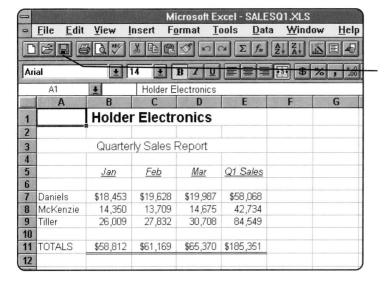

Your worksheet should now look like the example below.

7. Click on the **Save button** to save your work.

Program Manager

Part III: Multiple Worksheets and Formulas

Setting Up a Second Worksheet

Workbook files come with 16 tabs. Each tab represents a new worksheet. You can have up to 255 tabs in a single workbook. Can you imagine needing 255 tabs?! Tabs allow you to switch back and forth between worksheets. You can copy information from one worksheet to another. In this chapter, you will do the following:

❖ Add a second worksheet to a file

❖ Switch back and forth between two worksheets

❖ Copy data from one worksheet and paste it into a second worksheet

❖ Place names on worksheet tabs

ADDING A SECOND WORKSHEET

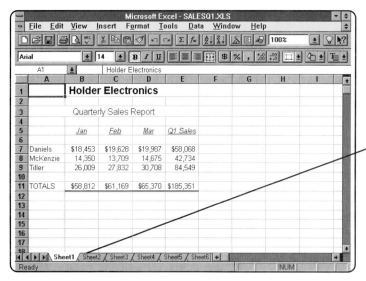

Because Excel workbooks are set up with 16 worksheets, you don't have to do anything to create additional worksheets. You simply click on the next tab.

1. **Click** on the **tab** for **Sheet2**. You will move to a blank worksheet.

SWITCHING BETWEEN WORKSHEETS

1. Click on the **Sheet1 tab**. You will go back to the Quarterly Sales Report worksheet.

You can move just as quickly through the entire 16 worksheets.

2. Click on the **outside right arrow** to move to the last tab in the workbook. Tabs for Sheets 12 through 16 will show at the bottom of your screen. (The outside arrows with the lines move you to the first and last tabs in the workbook. The inside arrows move you one tab at a time from where you are.)

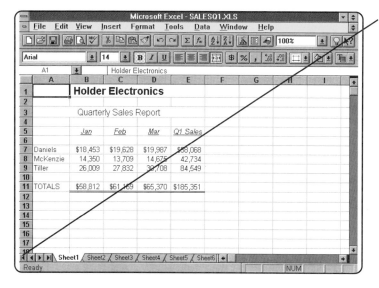

3. Click on the **outside left arrow** to show Sheet1.

COPYING BETWEEN WORKSHEETS

In this example, you will copy the heading from Sheet1 to Sheet2 using the Copy and Paste buttons.

Using the Copy Button

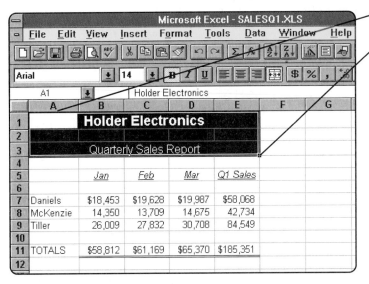

1. Click on **A1** on Sheet1.

2. Press and hold the mouse button and **drag** the highlight bar to **E3**.

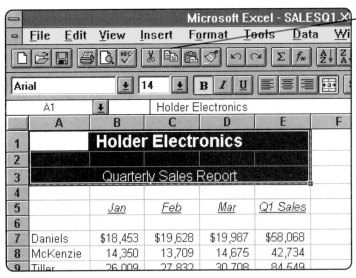

3. Click on the **Copy button** on the toolbar. You will see a moving border (sometimes affectionately called "running ants") around the highlighted text. The highlighted text has been copied to the Clipboard, a storage area that holds copied, deleted, or cleared data. The data will stay in the Clipboard until it is replaced with other data.

Using the Paste Button

1. **Click** on the **Sheet2 tab**.

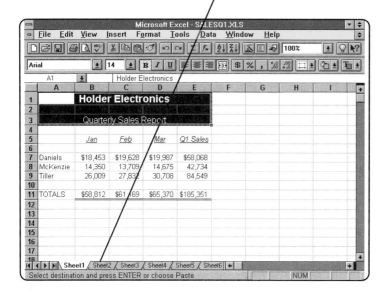

2. **Click** on **A1** on Sheet2.

3. **Click** on the **Paste button** on the toolbar. The copied information will appear on Sheet2 beginning at cell A1.

This heading is not exactly right for this worksheet. You will edit it in the next chapter.

4. Click on the **Sheet1 tab** to go back to Quarterly Sales Report.

Copying with the Shortcut Menu

In this example, you will copy the salespeople's names from Sheet1 using a shortcut menu.

1. Notice that the ants are still running. **Press** the **Esc key** on your keyboard and they'll disappear.

2. Click on Daniels in **A7**. Keep the pointer in the middle of the cell.

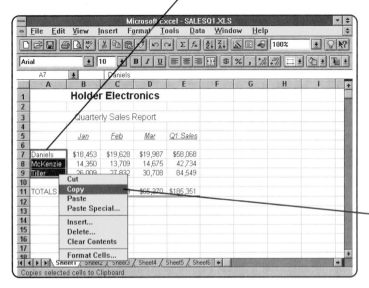

3. Press and hold the mouse button and **drag** the pointer down to Tiller in **A9**. All three names will be highlighted. Leave the pointer in the highlighted area.

4. Click the **right mouse button**. A shortcut menu will appear.

5. Click on **Copy**. The ants will appear again as the highlighted names are copied to the Clipboard.

Pasting with the Shortcut Menu

1. **Click** on the **Sheet2 tab**.

2. **Click** on **A6** on Sheet2. Leave the pointer in the cell.

3. **Click** the **right mouse button**. A shortcut menu will appear.

4. **Click** on **Paste**. The copied names will appear beginning in A6.

5. **Click anywhere** on the worksheet to remove the highlighting.

NAMING WORKSHEETS

You can put a worksheet name on each tab so that it's easier to remember what each worksheet is about. The name can have up to 31 characters, including spaces.

1. **Click twice** on the **Sheet2 tab**. A Rename Sheet dialog box will appear.

2. Type JanComm (for January Commission). It will replace the highlighted Sheet2.

3. Click on **OK**. "JanComm" will appear on the Sheet2 tab.

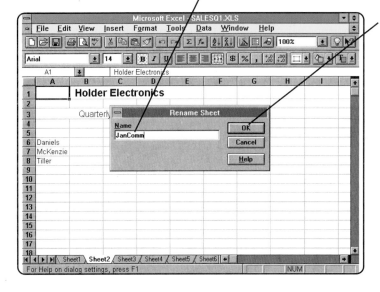

4. Click on the **Sheet1 tab** to make it the active worksheet. Now that Sheet1 is the active worksheet, you are ready for the next step.

Notice that the salespeoples' names are still highlighted and surrounded by the moving border.

5. Click anywhere on the worksheet to remove the highlighting and **press** the **Esc key** to remove the running ants.

6. Click twice on the **Sheet1 tab**. A Rename Sheet dialog box will appear.

7. **Type SalesQ1**. It will replace the highlighted Sheet1.

8. **Click** on **OK**. "SalesQ1" will appear on the Sheet1 tab.

9. **Click** on the **Save button** on the toolbar. Both SalesQ1 and JanComm will be saved in the SALESQ1.XLS workbook.

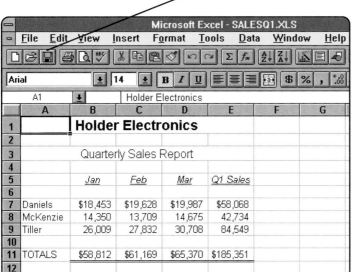

You will format the JanComm worksheet in the next chapter, "Formatting a Second Worksheet."

Formatting a Second Worksheet

You can preformat an entire worksheet so that numbers appear in a specified style. In addition to the standard Windows functions of copying and pasting, Excel has a feature, called drag-and-drop moving, that will come in handy as you format the second worksheet. In this chapter, you will do the following:

❖ Preformat the worksheet so that all numbers appear in a specific format

❖ Move data on a worksheet with drag-and-drop moving

❖ Use Text Wrap to put two lines in a cell

EDITING COPIED DATA

In this section, you will change the report name to "January Commission Report."

1. **Click** on the **JanComm tab** to move to that worksheet.

2. **Click twice** on **A3** to open the cell for in-cell editing.

3. Place the cursor at the **beginning** of the cell. It will change to an I-beam.

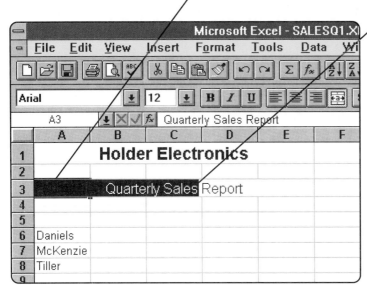

4. Press and hold the mouse button and **drag** the highlight bar over **Quarterly Sales**. Make sure that you don't highlight the space after "Sales" or you will delete the space between the words when you make the correction.

5. Type January Commission. It will replace the highlighted text.

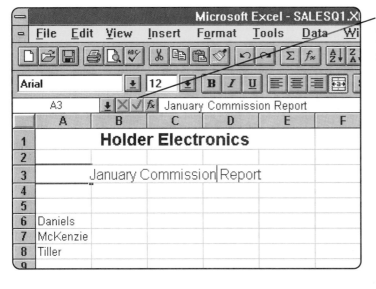

6. Click on ✔ (or press Enter) to enter the change in the cell.

PREFORMATTING NUMBERS

In this section, you will set up the worksheet so that every number entered will appear with a comma when appropriate.

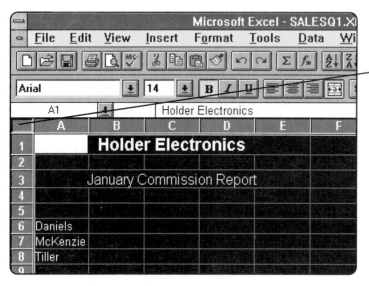

1. **Click** on the **Select All button** at the intersection of the column letters and row numbers. The entire worksheet will be highlighted in black with the exception of the first cell in the range, which will remain white.

2. **Click** on **Format** in the menu bar. A pull-down menu will appear.

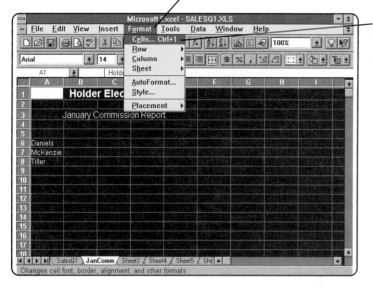

3. **Click** on **Cells**. The Format Cells dialog box will appear.

4. Click on the **Number tab** if it is not already in front.

5. Click on **Number** in the Category box.

6. Click on **#,##0**, which is the third choice on the Format Codes list.

7. Click on **OK**. Any number entered into the worksheet will appear with a comma and no decimal places. You will modify the formatting in certain columns later in this chapter.

DRAG-AND-DROP MOVING

If you followed the steps in Chapter 11, you copied the heading and the salespeople's names from the SalesQ1 worksheet to the JanComm worksheet. If not, you will need to follow the steps in the section "Copying Between Worksheets," in Chapter 11, before you do these procedures. In this section, you will move McKenzie and Tiller.

1. Click on McKenzie in **A7**.

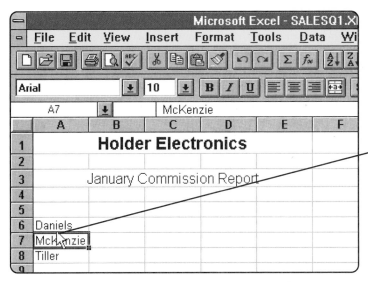

2. Move the **pointer** to the **top border** of the cell. The pointer will become an arrow. You may have to fiddle with the placement of the pointer so that it stays an arrow.

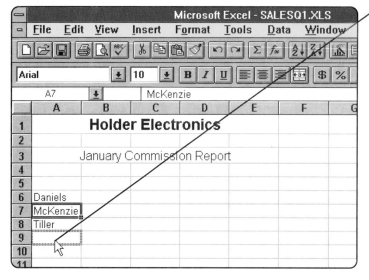

3. Press and hold the mouse button and **drag** McKenzie down to **A9**. You will see a gray outline being dragged.

4. Release the mouse button when the outline is in A9. McKenzie will appear in A9.

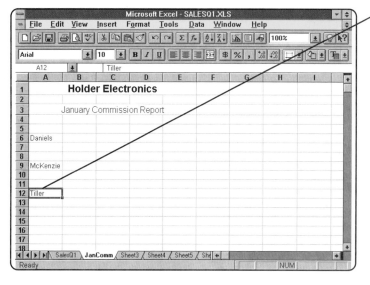

5. Click on Tiller in **A8** and **repeat steps 2 through 4** to **move Tiller to A12**.

ADDING TEXT WRAP TO A ROW

Using the Text Wrap feature allows you to divide a long entry into two lines. In this section, you will set up row 5 to wrap text so that column headings will appear as two lines.

1. **Click** on the **row 5 button**. The entire row will be highlighted with the exception of the first cell, which will be white. leave the pointer in the highlighted row.

2. **Click** the **right mouse button**. A shortcut menu will appear.

3. **Click** on **Format Cells**. The Format Cells dialog box will appear.

4. **Click** on the **Alignment tab** to bring it to the front.

5. **Click** on **Wrap Text** to put an ✕ in the box.

6. **Click** on **OK**.

Entering Column Headings

1. **Type Salesperson** in **A5**. (It will wrap to a second line. Don't be concerned. You'll fix it later.) **Press** the → **key** on your keyboard to enter "Salesperson" and move to B5.

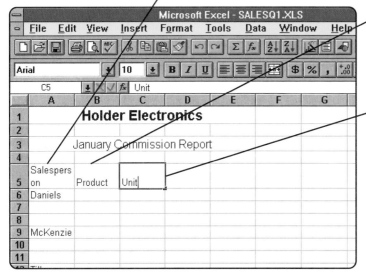

2. **Type Product** in **B5**. (Notice that it appears at the bottom of the cell.) **Press** the → **key** on your keyboard.

3. **Type Unit**.

4. **Press and hold** the **Alt key** and **press** the **Enter key** (Alt + Enter). This step tells Excel that you want to wrap at this exact point.

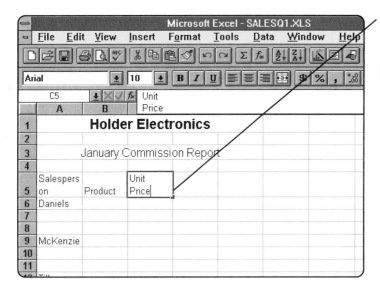

5. **Type Price**.

6. **Press** the → **key** on your keyboard to move to D5.

7. **Repeat** the directions in **steps 3 through 5** and **type Number Sold** on two lines in **D5**. Press **the → key** to move to E5.

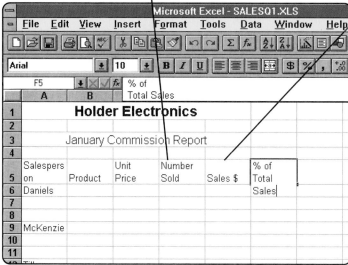

8. **Type Sales $** in E5 and **press** the **→ key** to move the F5.

9. **Repeat** the directions in **steps 3 through 5** and **type:**

> **% of**
> **Total Sales**

in cell **F5**. Notice that the entry takes up three lines even though you typed it on two lines. You will fix this later.

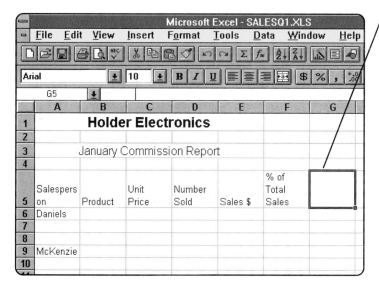

10. **Press** the **→ key** to move to **G5**.

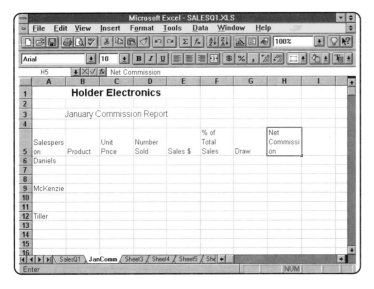

11. Type Draw and **press** the → **key** to move to H5.

12. Type Net Commission and **Press Enter**. You will fix the spacing in the next section.

CHANGING MULTIPLE COLUMN WIDTHS

In this section, you will fix the column headings from the previous section. You can apply a single command to non-adjacent columns by using the Ctrl key when you select the columns.

1. Click on **A** in the first column heading. The entire column will be highlighted.

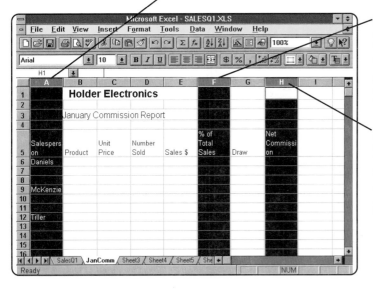

2. Press and hold the **Ctrl key** and **click** on the column heading for **F**. The entire column will be highlighted.

3. Press and hold the **Ctrl key** and **click** on the column heading for **H**. All three columns will be highlighted.

4. Click on **Format** in the menu bar. A pull-down menu will appear.

5. Click on **Column**. A second menu will appear.

6. Click on **Width**. The Column Width dialog box will appear.

7. Type 11. It will be entered in the width box.

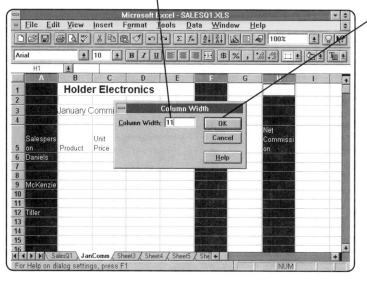

8. Click on **OK**. The highlighted columns will be changed to an 11-character width.

CENTERING TEXT IN A ROW

In this example, you will highlight row 5 and apply a centering command to all of the cells in the row.

1. **Click** on the **row 5 button**. The entire row will be highlighted.

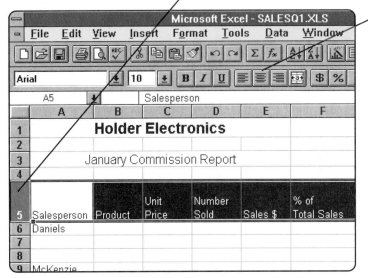

2. **Click** on the **Center button** in the toolbar. The text in each cell in row 5 will be centered.

RECENTERING THE HEADING

Notice that the heading you copied from the first worksheet is not centered over this second worksheet. Fortunately, it's easy to fix.

1. **Click** on **A1**.

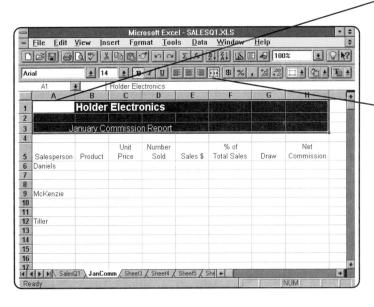

2. **Press and hold** the mouse button and **drag** the highlight bar to **H3**.

3. **Click twice** on the **Center Across Columns button** on the toolbar. The first click will take off the centering and move the text to column A. The second click will reapply the centering command. The text will be centered across all the columns.

REPEATING THE CONTENTS OF A CELL WITH AUTOFILL

1. Click on Daniels in **A6**.

2. Click and hold on the **fill button** in the bottom right corner of the cell and **drag** the border down to **A8**.

3. Release the mouse button and "Daniels" will be repeated in all three cells.

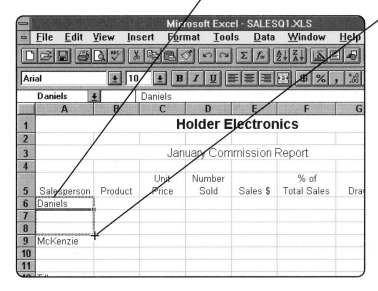

4. Repeat steps 1 through 3 to repeat **McKenzie** in A10 and A11.

5. Repeat steps 1 through 3 to repeat **Tiller** in A13 and A14.

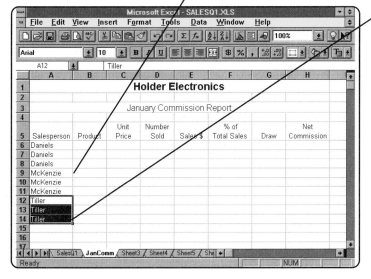

OVERRIDING NUMBER FORMATS

Although you have preformatted the worksheet to have commas and no decimal places, you can apply a style to override this formatting. In this example, you will apply the Comma style to column C. This step will put two decimal places in the column.

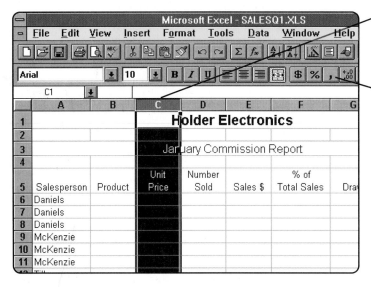

1. Click on the **column C button**. The entire column will be highlighted.

2. Click on the **Comma button** in the toolbar. You won't see any change in the screen, but the column is now formatted for two decimal places.

COPYING AND PASTING A RANGE

In this section, you will enter text into six cells. Then you will copy and paste the text into other cells.

Entering Text

1. Click on **B6.**

2. Type the letter **A** and **press Enter.** The border will move to B7.

3. **Repeat step 2** and **type** the letters **B** and **C** in **B7** and **B8**.

4. **Click** on **C6**.

5. **Type 1.5** and **press Enter**. The border will move to C7 and 1.50 will be entered into the cell because you formatted this column to have two decimal places.

6. **Repeat step 5** and **type 2** and **3** in cells **C7** and **C8**, respectively.

Copying a Range of Cells

1. **Click** on **B6**. Leave the pointer in the middle of the cell.

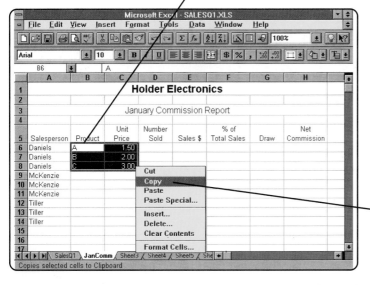

2. **Press and hold** the mouse button and **drag** the pointer down to **B8** and over to **C8**. Leave the pointer in the highlighted area.

3. **Click** the **right mouse button**. A shortcut menu will appear.

4. **Click** on **Copy**. The highlighted cells will be surrounded by a moving border.

Pasting a Range of Cells

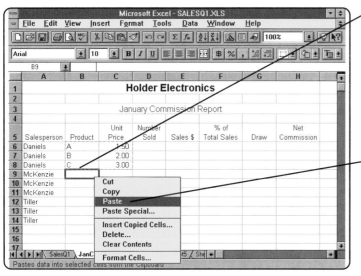

1. **Click** on **B9**. On your screen, it will be empty. Leave the pointer in the cell.

2. **Click** the **right mouse button**. A shortcut menu will appear.

3. **Click** on **Paste**. The contents of the highlighted cells will be copied into B9 through C11.

4. **Repeat steps 1 through 3** to paste the data into **B12** through **C14**. (Because the copied data is still in the Clipboard and has not been replaced with data from another Copy or Delete command, you can paste it again.)

5. **Press** the **Esc key** to stop the running ants in the border.

ENTERING NUMBERS

In this example, you will enter the number sold for each product.

1. Enter the following numbers in column D:

3702 in D6

5550 in D7

600 in D8

3284 in D9

3587 in D10

750 in D11

3670 in D12

8902 in D13

900 in D14

Save Your Work

1. Click on the **Save button** to save your work.

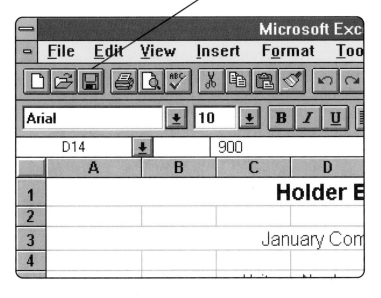

Writing Formulas and Using the Subtotal Feature

Writing formulas is a breeze in Excel 5. You use standard symbols for mathematical processes. Addition is symbolized by a plus sign (+); subtraction by a hyphen (-); multiplication by an asterisk (*); and division by a forward slash (/). Excel 5 has an exciting new feature, called Subtotal, that will reformat your worksheet and insert authomatically subtotals and a grand total. In this chapter, you will do the following:

❖ Use the Subtotal feature

❖ Write formulas for multiplication, division, subtraction, and percentage

❖ Copy formulas to other cells

WRITING A MULTIPLICATION FORMULA

In this section, you will write a formula to calculate Sales $ = Unit Price x Number Sold.

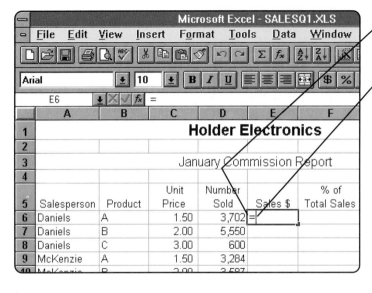

1. Click on **E6**. On your screen, it will be empty.

2. Type = to tell Excel that you are starting a formula. The = will appear in the formula bar and in the cell.

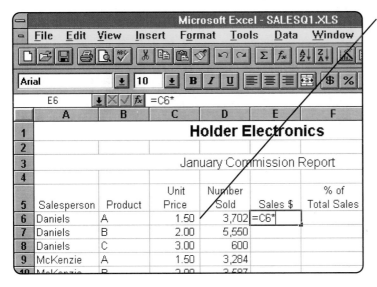

3. Click on 1.50 in **C6**. A running border will appear around the cell, and C6 will appear in the formula bar and in E6.

4. Type * (the symbol for multiplication). The running border will disappear. The * will appear in the formula bar and in E6.

5. Click on **D6**. A running border will appear around the cell, and D6 will appear in the formula bar and in E6. The formula reads "=C6*D6."

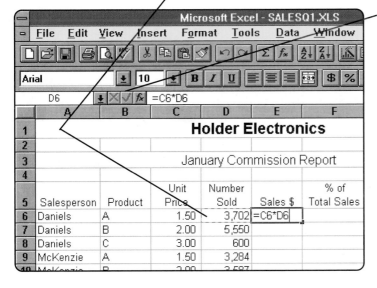

6. Click on ✔. The results of the multiplication formula (5,553) will appear in E6.

COPYING A FORMULA

In this example, you will use the multitalented AutoFill feature to copy the multiplication formula in E6 to the rest of the cells in the column.

1. Click on **E6** if it is not already selected.

2. Place the **pointer** on top of the **fill handle** in the lower-right corner of the cell. The pointer will change to a black plus sign.

3. Click and hold on the fill handle and **drag** it down the column to **E14**. You will see a gray border surround the cells.

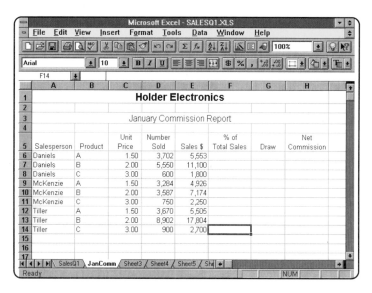

4. Release the mouse button when the border extends down to E14. The formula will be copied into each cell, and the resulting totals will appear.

5. Click anywhere on the worksheet to remove the highlighting.

A NOTE ABOUT FORMULAS

In the previous section, you were able to copy the multiplication formula to different rows because the cells in the new rows are in the same pattern as the cells in the original row. You multiply the number in column C by the number in column D to get the answer in column E regardless of the row. When you copy this kind of formula, Excel automatically adjusts the cell reference to reflect the new row.

When you created the multiplication formula in E6, it read "=C6*D6." When you copied the formula, Excel changed the row numbers. Try the following steps to see how the cell reference changes in each row.

1. Click twice on **E7**.

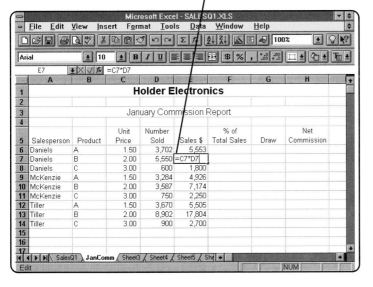

Notice that the formula in the cell reads "=C7*D7" to reflect that the formula was copied into row 7.

2. Click on the **next cell** to remove the in-cell editing function from E7.

3. Repeat steps 1 and 2 to see the formula in some of the other cells in column E. Each cell will have a formula that reflects the appropriate row.

CREATING SUBTOTALS

The Subtotal feature is one of the exciting new features in Excel 5. It will automatically insert and label total rows and calculate subtotals and grand totals. To use the Subtotal feature, your data must have column labels (Salesperson, Product, or Unit Price, for example).

Your screen may have scrolled so that column A does not show.

1. Click on the ⬅ on the bottom scroll bar to bring column A into view if you cannot see it.

2. Click on Salesperson in **A5**. Leave the pointer in the cell.

3. Press and hold the mouse button and **drag** the pointer down to **E14**. Although you can highlight all of the columns if you want Excel to put subtotals in them, in this example you will include only columns A through E.

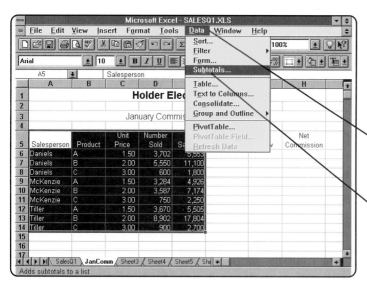

4. Click on **Data** in the menu bar. A pull-down menu will appear.

5. Click on **Subtotals**. The Subtotal dialog box will appear.

6. Confirm that **Salesperson** shows in the At Each Change In box.

7. Confirm that **Sum** is in the Use Function box.

8. Confirm that **Sales $** has an ✕ in the box. Sales $ is selected because this is the last column in the highlighted area. Excel automatically assumes that you want to have totals in the last column. Notice that the items in this list are your column headings. Although you can choose to have subtotals for other column headings, in this example, you will select only Sales $.

9. Click on **OK**. The worksheet will be reformatted.

10. Click on the ⬇ on the scroll bar to show row 18 on the worksheet.

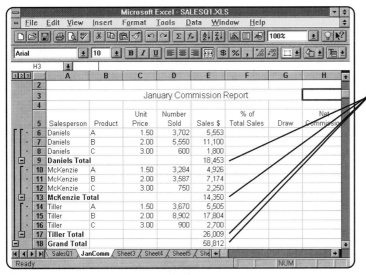

11. Click anywhere on the worksheet to remove the highlighting.

Notice that summary lines have been added for each salesperson and the totals automatically calculated.

WRITING A
DIVISION FORMULA

In this section, you will write a formula to calculate % of Total Sales = Salesperson's Total ÷ Grand Total.

1. Click on **F9**. On your screen, it will be blank.

2. Type = to tell Excel you are starting a formula.

3. Click on 18,453 in **E9**. A moving border will appear around the cell.

4. Type / (a forward slash), the symbol for division.

5. Type $E$18. Inserting the $s in the cell reference creates an *absolute cell reference*. This tells Excel it *must* use E18 as the divisor. It cannot modify this cell reference when you copy the formula.

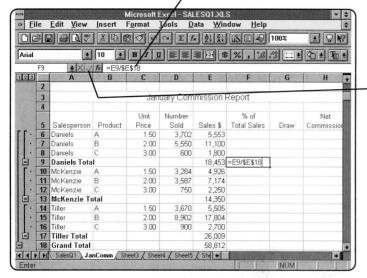

6. Click on the ✔. Notice that a 0 appears in F9! The worksheet is formatted for commas and no decimal places; therefore, Excel can't show the result of the formula in this cell because it is a decimal. Now you have to format the column to show a percent.

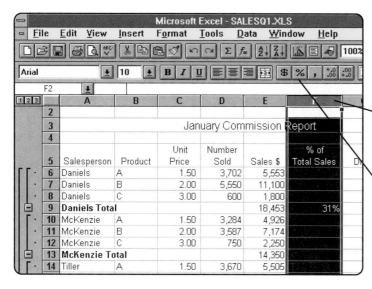

Formatting a Column for Percents

1. **Click** on the **column F** heading. The entire column will be highlighted.

2. **Click** on the **% button** in the toolbar. "31%" will appear in F9.

Copying a Formula with Drag and Drop

Because you wrote the division formula using an absolute cell reference, you can copy it to other rows and Excel will not modify the cell reference to match the row number as it did in the multiplication formula.

1. **Click** on F9. **Place** the mouse pointer on the **border of the cell**. It will change to an arrow.

2. **Press and hold** the **Ctrl key**. A tiny plus sign will appear.

3. **Continue to hold** the **Ctrl key** and **drag** the cell border to **F13**. Release the mouse **first** then release the Ctrl key. 24% will appear in F13.

4. **Repeat steps 1 through 3** to copy the formula into F17. 44% will appear in F17.

COPYING NUMBERS

In preparation for writing the subtraction formula, you will enter the amount Daniels receives as a draw against commission and then copy that amount to the other salespeople.

1. **Click** on **G9**.

2. **Type 1000** and **click ✔**. Leave the pointer in the cell.

3. **Click** the **right mouse button**. A shortcut menu will appear.

4. **Click** on **Copy**. The number is now copied to the Clipboard.

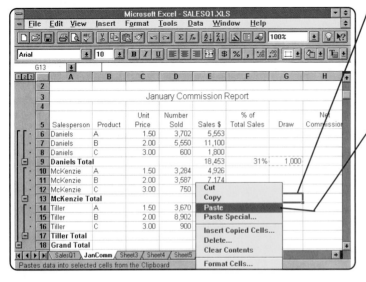

5. **Click** on **G13**. Leave the pointer in the cell.

6. **Click** the **right mouse button**. A shortcut menu will appear.

7. **Click** on **Paste** and 1,000 will appear in G13.

8. **Repeat steps 5 through 7** to **enter 1,000** in **G17**.

9. **Press** the **Esc key** to stop the moving border around G9.

WRITING A FORMULA WITH TWO OPERATIONS

In this section, you will write a formula to calculate Net Commission = Sales $ - Draw. This calculation requires that you multiply the Sales $ by a 15% commission and then subtract the draw amount.

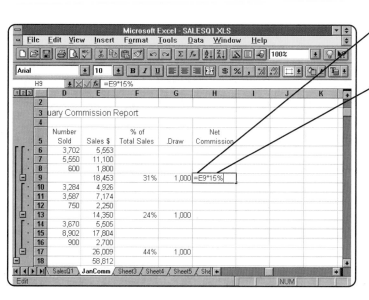

1. Click on the ➡ on the scroll bar to bring column H into full view.

2. Click on **H9**.

3. Type = to start a formula.

4. Click on 18,453 in **E9**.

5. Type an **asterisk** (*), the symbol for multiplication.

6. Type 15%, the percent these salespeople receive as commission. (You can enter a percent as a decimal or with the percent sign.)

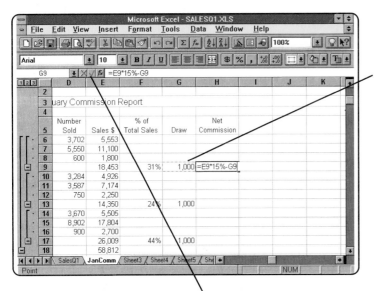

7. Type a **hyphen (-)**, the symbol for subtraction.

8. Click on 1,000 in **G9**.

9. **Click** on ✔. Excel will calculate 15% of Daniels' total sales and then subtract 1,000.

You will see 1,768 appear in H9.

You can copy this formula to other rows because the cells in the new rows are in the same pattern as the cells in row 9.

Before you copy this formula, however, there are a few details about formulas you should know.

MORE ABOUT FORMULAS

Formulas in Excel can be as simple or as complex as you like. However, most will contain the basic arithmetic operations of addition, subtraction, multiplication, and division.

If you include more than one operation in a formula, Excel performs them in the order shown to the left.

For example, in the formula 10-2*3, the * is performed first, giving a product of 6. Then the subtraction is performed, giving a final answer of 4.

Putting parentheses in a formula will cause Excel to perform the calculation within the parentheses before all others. When a set of parentheses is inside another set of parentheses, the calculation of the inside parentheses is performed first and then the calculation required by the outside parentheses. Within parentheses, the precedence order above applies. Look at the order in which the functions are performed in the following example:

Arithmetic operations are performed in the following order:

1. * Multiplication
2. / Division
3. + Addition
4. - Subtraction

```
325 + ((500 + B7) * 4) / 8 - E25
 |        |        |    |    |
4th      1st      2nd  3rd  5th
```

This example has spaces added simply to make the explanation easier to see. When you write formulas, do not put spaces before or after the operation symbols.

Consult the *User's Guide* that came with your software for a thorough discussion of formulas.

Copying the Formula

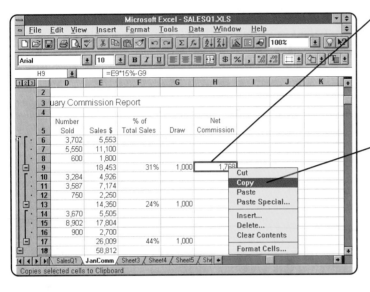

1. Click on **H9** and leave the pointer in the cell.

2. Click the **right mouse button**. A shortcut menu will appear.

3. Click on **Copy**. The formula will be copied.

4. Click on **H13** and leave the pointer in the cell.

5. Click the **right mouse button** to bring up the shortcut menu.

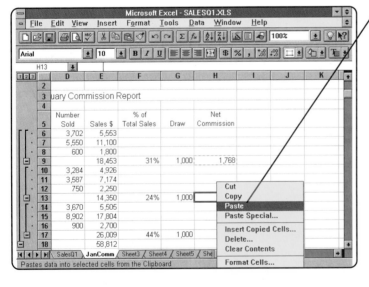

6. Click on **Paste**. The formula will be pasted in the cell and 1,153 will appear.

7. Repeat steps 4 through 6 to paste the formula into **H17**. You will see "2,901" appear in the cell.

8. Press the **Esc key** to stop the moving border around H9.

USING AUTOSUM WITH NONADJACENT CELLS

In this example, you will use the AutoSum button to add the three numbers in column H.

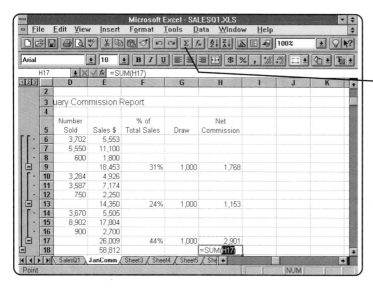

1. **Click** on **H18**. On your screen, it will be empty.

2. **Click** on the **AutoSum button** in the toolbar.

Notice that the formula in H18 is "=SUM(H17)." This means that it will add only H17 into the total. You can tell Excel to include other cells by highlighting them.

3. **Click** on **H9**. Leave the pointer in the cell.

4. **Press and hold** the mouse button and **drag** the pointer down to **H17**. Cells H9 through H17 will be surrounded by a moving border. The formula in H18 will read "=SUM(H9:H17)."

5. **Click** on ✔. The sum 5,882 will appear in H18.

USING THE OUTLINE SYMBOLS IN SUBTOTAL

When you applied Subtotal to the JanComm worksheet, Excel added the outline symbols in the gray area to the left of the worksheet. These symbols are used to "collapse" the worksheet to show various levels of summary data.

1. Click on the ← on the scroll bar to bring column A into view.

2. Click on the **level 1 outline symbol**. The worksheet will be collapsed to show only the Grand Total.

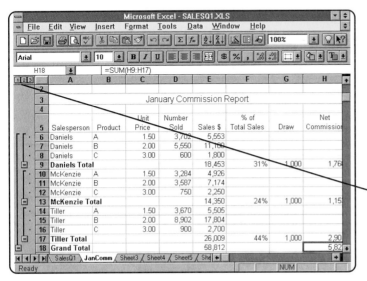

3. Click on the **level 2 outline symbol**. The worksheet will show only the Subtotal amounts and the Grand Total.

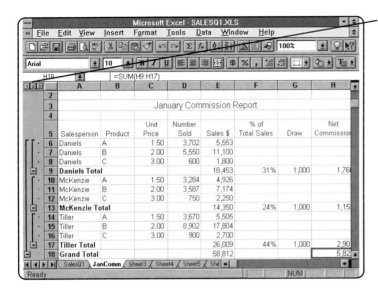

4. Click on the **level 3 outline symbol**. The worksheet will be fully expanded.

Your worksheet will look like this example.

Save Your Work

1. Click on the **Save button** in the toolbar to save your work.

Using AutoFormat

AutoFormat is another of Excel's special features. It contains a selection of predesigned formats you can apply to your worksheet. You can even modify an AutoFormat style. In this chapter, you will do the following:

❖ Apply an AutoFormat style
❖ Remove an AutoFormat style
❖ Modify the predesigned style

SELECTING AN AUTOFORMAT STYLE

In this section, you will choose an AutoFormat style and apply it to the JanComm worksheet. In this example, you will not change the style of the heading; therefore, you will not include it in the range of cells to be styled.

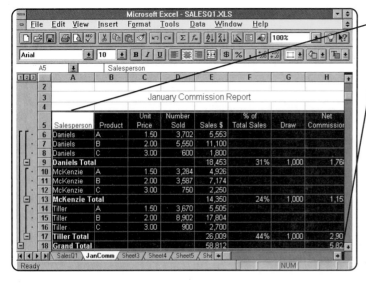

1. Click on **A5**. Leave the pointer in the cell.

2. Press and hold the mouse button and **drag** the highlight bar over to **H5** and down to **H18**. **Release** the mouse button when rows 5 through 18 are highlighted.

3. **Click** on **Format** in the menu bar. A pull-down menu will appear.

4. **Click** on **AutoFormat**. The AutoFormat dialog box will appear.

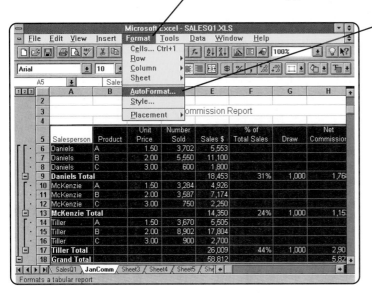

The AutoFormat dialog box contains a list of 16 formats you can apply to your worksheet.

As you click on each choice in the Table Format list, the Sample box will show what the format looks like. Click on a few of the choices to see what they look like. After you've seen the selections, go on to step 5.

5. **Click** on **Classic 2**.

6. **Click** on **Options**. The AutoFormat dialog box will be expanded to include Formats to Apply.

CUSTOMIZING AN AUTOFORMAT STYLE

If you like a particular AutoFormat style, you can customize it so that it doesn't override any formatting you have already applied to your worksheet.

1. Click on **Number** to remove the ✕ from the box.

2. Click on **Alignment** to remove the ✕ from the box.

3. Click on **Width/Height** to remove the ✕ from the box.

The number formatting, alignment, and width and height of cells will now remain as you set them even after the Classic2 style is applied to the worksheet.

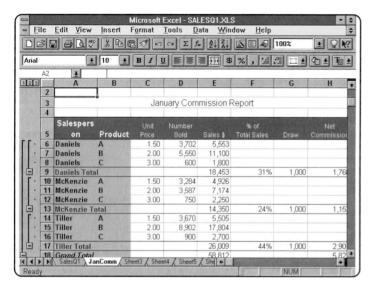

4. Click on **OK**. The dialog box will close and the Classic2 style will be applied to the worksheet.

The color on the worksheet is a little strange, but it will change when you remove the highlighting.

5. Click anywhere on the worksheet to remove the highlighting.

REMOVING AN AUTOFORMAT STYLE

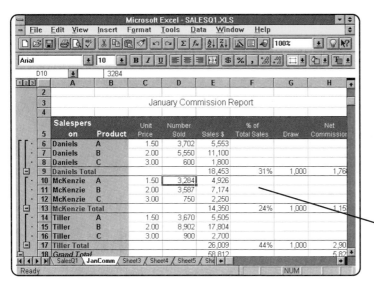

You can use the Undo button to remove an AutoFormat style if you use it immediately after you apply the style. If you have performed any other function, however, you will have to do the following steps to remove the AutoFormat style.

1. Click anywhere in the formatted range of cells.

2. Click on **Format** in the menu bar. A pull-down menu will appear.

3. Click on **AutoFormat**. The AutoFormat dialog box will appear.

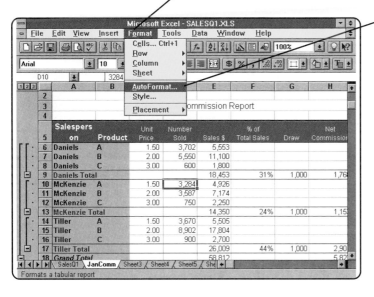

4. Click and hold the **button** on the scroll bar and **drag** it down to the bottom of the scroll bar.

5. Click on **None**.

6. Click on **OK**. The worksheet will reappear with the AutoFormat style removed.

Notice that this step removed all the styles from the worksheet. You can reapply the styles or you can do the following step:

7. Click on the **Undo button** in the toolbar. The Classic2 AutoFormat style will be restored.

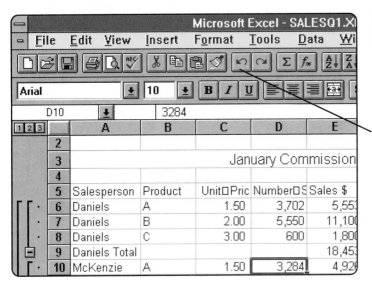

MODIFYING AN APPLIED AUTOFORMAT STYLE

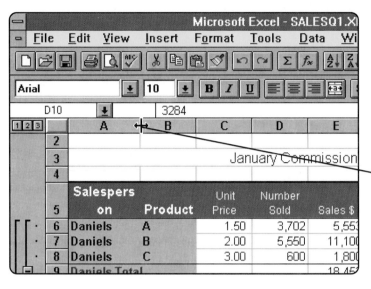

You modify an applied AutoFormat style the same way you apply any style to a cell, column, or row. In this example, you will increase the width of column A so that Salesperson appears on one line.

1. **Place** the mouse pointer on the **line between the column A and column B headers**. The pointer will change to the shape you see in this example.

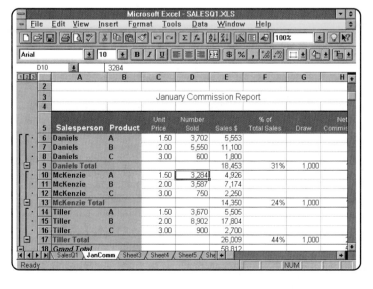

2. **Click twice**. The column will expand to a best-fit width.

The worksheet will look like this example.

Working with Large Worksheets

When you work with a large worksheet, it is annoying to watch the column and row headings scroll out of sight. Excel solves this problem by letting you freeze parts of your worksheet into separate sections, or *panes*, which always remain in view. It also lets you change the view so that more of your worksheet is visible on your screen. In this chapter, you will do the following:

❖ Freeze and unfreeze a row and column (panes)

❖ Change the view (zoom out) so that you can see more of the worksheet on your screen

❖ Zoom in to magnify a portion of the worksheet

FREEZING COLUMNS AND ROWS

In this section, you will freeze the JanComm worksheet so that row 5 and columns A and B are always visible. Because you do not need to have "Holder Electronics" and "January Commission Report" on your screen at all times, you can scroll these names out of sight before you freeze the worksheet.

Going Home

1. Press the **Home key** on your keyboard to move to A1. If the Home key doesn't take you to A1, press Ctrl + Home.

2. Click on the ⬇ on the scroll bar until rows 1 through 4 have scrolled out of sight.

Selecting the Freezing Point

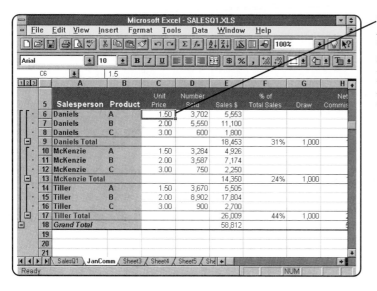

1. Click on **C6**. This will become the freezing point and cells above it and to the left of it will stay frozen on your screen.

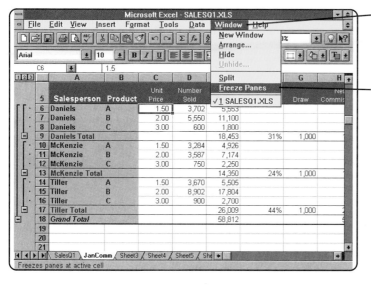

2. Click on **Window** in the menu bar. A pull-down menu will appear.

3. Click on **Freeze Panes**.

Notice the freeze lines on the worksheet. The horizontal line is hard to see because of the colored heading, but it's there.

Scrolling in a Frozen Worksheet

1. Click twice on the ↓ on the scroll bar to scroll down the worksheet.

Notice that the headings in row 5 remain in view even though rows 6 and 7 have scrolled out of sight.

2. Click twice on the → on the bottom scroll bar to scroll to the right in the worksheet.

Notice that columns A and B remain on your screen even though columns C and D have scrolled out of sight.

3. Click on **H18**.

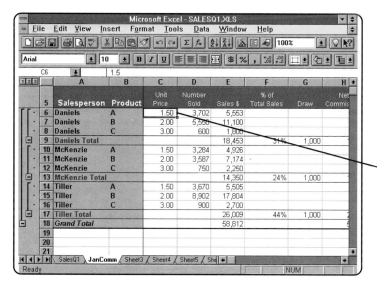

Going Home on a Frozen Screen

Normally when you press the Home key, you return to A1. When you have frozen your worksheet, you will return to the "freezing point," which in this example is C6.

1. Press the **Home key** (or Ctrl + Home) on your keyboard. The border will return to C6.

UNFREEZING PANES

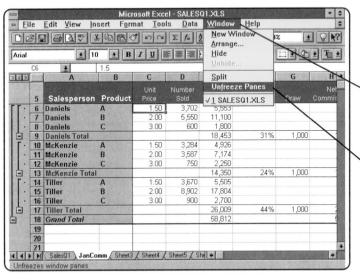

It doesn't matter where the selected cell is when you unfreeze panes.

1. Click on **Window** in the menu bar. A pull-down menu will appear.

2. Click on **Unfreeze Panes**. The freeze lines will be removed from the worksheet.

CHANGING THE SCREEN VIEW

The Zoom feature in Excel resembles the zoom lens on a camera. You can *zoom out* and fit more of the worksheet on the screen. Or you can *zoom in* and magnify a specific area.

Zooming Out

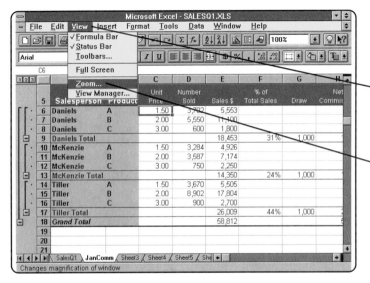

1. Click on **View** in the menu bar. A pull-down menu will appear.

2. Click on **Zoom**. The Zoom dialog box will appear.

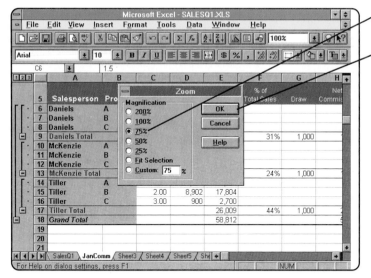

3. **Click** on **75%**.

4. **Click** on **OK**. You will zoom out to a view where the worksheet has shrunk to 75% of its normal size.

Zooming In

1. **Click** on **View** in the menu bar. A pull-down menu will appear.

2. **Click** on **Zoom**. The Zoom dialog box will appear.

3. **Click** on **200%**.

4. **Click** on **OK**. The worksheet will appear at 200% of its normal size.

Returning to the Normal View

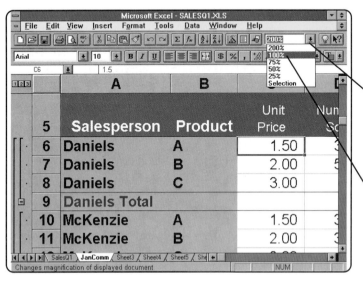

Excel has a button in the toolbar that makes changing views easy.

1. **Click** on the ⬇ to the right of the Zoom Control box. A drop-down list will appear.

2. **Click** on **100%**. The screen will return to the normal view.

Linking Two Worksheets

When you establish a *link* between two worksheets, any change made in the linked data on the first worksheet (the *source* worksheet) is immediately reflected in the linked data on the second worksheet (the *dependent* worksheet). The process of creating a link is very easy. In this chapter, you will do the following:

❖ Use JANCOMM.XLS as the source worksheet and open a new file as the dependent worksheet

❖ Arrange both worksheets on your screen at the same time

❖ Link the worksheets

❖ Test the link

GETTING READY TO LINK

In this section, you will use JANCOMM.XLS as the source worksheet because it contains the net commission data that will be transferred to a second worksheet. Then you will open a new file that will become the *dependent* worksheet and receive the data from the source worksheet. Open the SALESQ1 workbook and go to the Jancomm worksheet if you are not already there.

Opening a New Workbook

1. **Click** on **File** in the menu bar. A pull-down menu will appear.

2. **Click** on **New**. A new workbook will appear and cover up the SALESQ1 workbook.

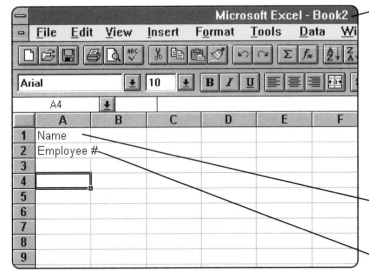

Notice Book2 in the title bar.

Entering Data in the New Workbook

1. Click on **A1**. On your screen, it will be blank.

2. Type Name and **press Enter**.

3. Type Employee # in A2 and **press Enter twice** to move to A4. Employee # is too long for the cell. You'll widen the column a little later.

4. Type Month and **press Enter** to move to A5.

Entering a Series of Months

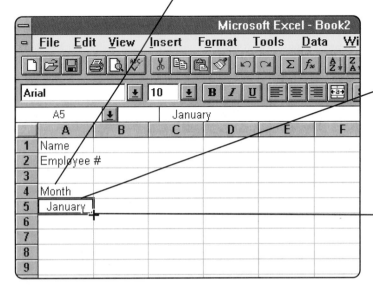

In this section, you will enter a series of months in Column A.

1. Press the **spacebar twice** and then **type January**. This step will indent "January" two spaces.

2. Click on ✔.

3. Place the pointer on the **fill handle** in the lower right corner of the cell border. It will become a black plus sign.

4. Press and hold the mouse button and **drag** the fill handle down to **A16**. The bottom border of the cell will expand as you drag.

5. Release the mouse button when you have included A5:A16 in the border outline. The series January through December will appear in the cells. Notice that the entire series is indented two spaces. If you dragged too far down column A and the series started to repeat itself, simply drag the fill handle up to remove the extra months.

6. Click anywhere to remove the highlighting.

Increasing Cell Width

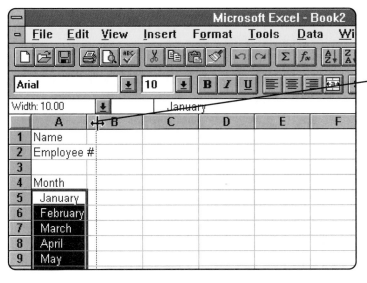

In this section, you will drag the mouse to increase the width of column A.

1. Place the pointer on the line **between columns A and B**. It will change to the shape you see in this example.

2. Press and hold the mouse button and **drag** the line to the **right**. The column will expand as you drag. **Release** the mouse button when the column is wide enough.

Entering a Number as Text

In this section, you will enter a name and employee number for Stacey Tiller. Because the employee number is for identification purposes only, you don't want Excel to treat it as an actual number. If you type an apostrophe before the number, Excel will treat it as text. The number will appear aligned on the left in the cell, like other text.

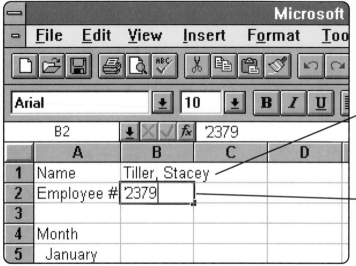

1. Click on **B1**. On your screen, it will be empty.

2. Type Tiller, Stacey and **press** the ↓ on your keyboard to enter the name in the cell and move to B2.

3. Type '2379. Don't forget the apostrophe. **Press Enter** to enter the number and move to the next cell.

Formatting the Worksheet

In this section, you will format the worksheet to have commas and two decimal places.

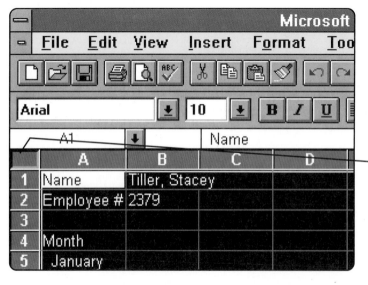

1. Click on the **Select All button** at the intersection of the row and column headings. The entire worksheet will be highlighted.

2. Click on **Format** in the menu bar. A pull-down menu will appear.

3. Click on **Cells**. The Format Cells dialog box will appear.

4. Click on the **Number tab** to bring it to the front if it is not already there.

5. Click on **Number** in the Category list.

6. Click on **#,##0.00**, which is the fourth option in the Format Codes list.

7. Click on **OK**. The dialog box will close. Any number entered into this worksheet will appear with a comma and two decimal places.

8. When the worksheet appears, **click anywhere** to remove the highlighting.

SWITCHING BETWEEN FILES

You can easily move back and forth between open files.

1. Click on **Window** in the menu bar. A pull-down menu will apprear.

Notice that the pull-down menu lists all open files at the bottom.

2. Click on **SALESQ1.XLS** and it will come to the foreground on your screen.

SHOWING TWO FILES AT THE SAME TIME

Now that the new worksheet is formatted, you are ready to make the link. The easiest way to begin linking two worksheets is to first arrange them on your screen so you can see them both at the same time. This, however, is not a prerequisite to linking.

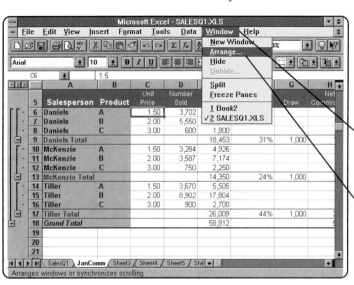

1. Click on **Window** in the menu bar. A pull-down menu will appear.

2. Click on **Arrange**. The Arrange Windows dialog box will appear.

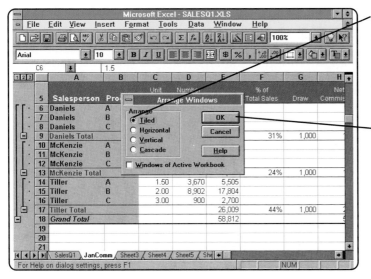

3. **Click** on **Tiled** if it does not already have a dot in the circle. This step will make the files appear side by side on the screen.

4. **Click** on **OK**.

The file that was visible on your screen when you performed the tile command is the active file in the tile arrangement. The active window has the brighter-colored title bar. The colors you see on your screen depend on the colors you set in Windows. Refer to *Windows 3.1: The Visual Learning Guide* for step-by-step directions on changing the colors on your screen.

MAKING THE LINK

Making the actual link between worksheets is the easiest part of the process.

1. **Click** on the ➡ on the scroll bar of SALESQ1 until you can see column H.

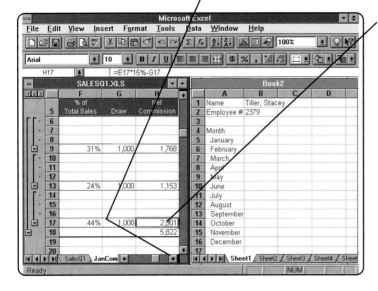

2. **Click** on 2,901 in **H17**. Leave the pointer in the cell.

3. **Click** the **right mouse button**. A shortcut menu will appear.

4. **Click** on **Copy**. The contents of the cell will be copied to the Clipboard.

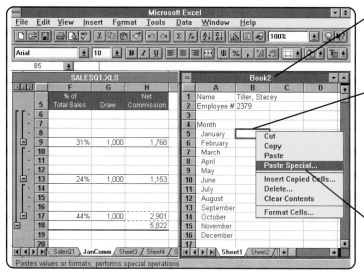

5. Click on the **Book2 title bar** to make it the active worksheet.

6. Click on **B5**. Leave the pointer in the cell.

7. Click the **right mouse button**. A shortcut menu will appear.

8. Click on **Paste Special**. The Paste Special dialog box will appear.

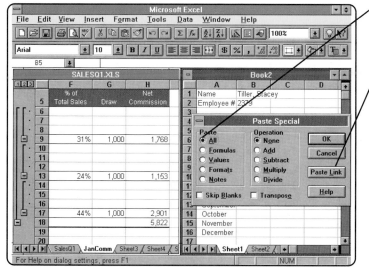

9. Click on **All** if it does not already have a dot in the circle.

10. Click on **Paste Link**. The dialog box will close and the number from the first worksheet will be linked into the second worksheet.

Notice that the number appears with two decimal places although it had no decimal places on the source worksheet. The reason is that you formatted the dependent worksheet to have two decimal places. When the format of the source and dependent worksheets are different, the format of the dependent worksheet controls the appearance of the data in the dependent worksheet.

The equal sign (=) at the beginning of the formula bar tells you that this cell is the result of a formula.

[SALESQ1.XLS] in the formula bar shows that this cell is the result of a formula in the SALESQ1 workbook. JanComm tells you the worksheet name. The exclamation point (!) means that it is a linked cell. The dollar signs ($H$17) indicate that Excel will always look in this specific cell in the source worksheet for the data to link to the dependent worksheet. This is called an *absolute cell reference.*

In the next section, you will have a little fun and test the link. You can do this by changing the Net Commission amount on SALESQ1 and then watching the change reflected in the linked data in the dependent worksheet. However, you cannot simply change the Net Commission amount because it is the result of a formula. You must change one of the numbers that is part of the formula. Then the Net commission amount will change. It gets a little complicated, doesn't it?

TESTING THE LINK

In this section, you will change the Draw amount on the source worksheet and watch as it affects the data in the dependent worksheet.

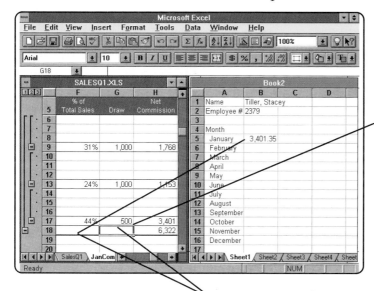

1. **Click** on the **title bar** of the SALESQ1 worksheet to make it the active worksheet.

2. **Click twice** on **G17** to open the cell for in-cell editing. On your screen 1,000 will be in G17.

3. **Click twice** again to highlight the contents of the cell.

4. **Type 500** and **press Enter** to insert the new number into G17. Watch as B5 on the new worksheet changes to 3,401.35.

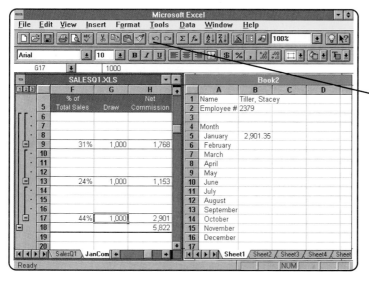

Undoing the Change

1. **Click** on the **Undo button** in the toolbar to undo the change. The original numbers will appear.

CLOSING WITHOUT SAVING

Because the unnamed Book2 was opened only to demonstrate the linking process, you will close it without saving.

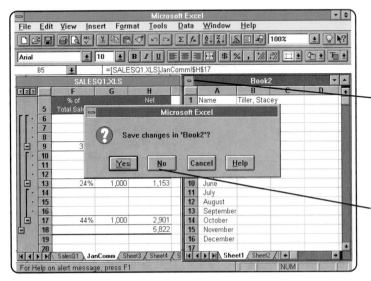

1. Click on the **Book2 title bar** to make it the active worksheet.

2. Click twice on the **Control menu box** ($\boxminus$) in the Book2 title bar. The Close dialog box will appear.

3. Click on **No**. The file will close. Because you never saved this file, the work you did in this file is gone.

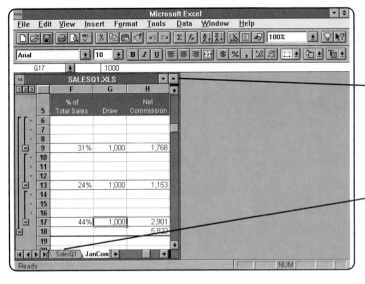

Maximizing the Remaining File

1. Click on the **Maximize button** (▲) on the SALESQ1 title bar. The worksheet will be maximized to fill the screen.

2. Click on the **SalesQ1 tab** in preparation for Chapter 17.

Program Manager

Part IV: Charts

Creating a 3-D Column Chart

With Excel 5's ChartWizard, you can create a chart (a graphic representation of your worksheet) automatically. You can select from a number of predesigned formats, including 3-D bar, line, pie, or area charts. After the chart is created, you can easily change it to another type. In this chapter, you will do the following:

❖ Create a simple column chart using the ChartWizard

❖ Add a chart title and legend

❖ Add category and value titles

❖ Change the column chart to a 3-D column chart

❖ Change the colors of the chart's bars

❖ Save the chart with the worksheet

USING THE CHARTWIZARD

1. **Open** the **SALESQ1 worksheet** you created in Part I and Part II. Refer to Chapter 7, "Opening a Saved Workbook," if you need help.

2. **Move** the mouse pointer to **A5**.

3. **Press and hold** the mouse button as you **drag** the **pointer** diagonally down to **D9**. **Release** the mouse button when you have highlighted the salespeoples' names and the sales data for Jan, Feb, and Mar (cells A5 through D9). Do not highlight the totals in column E and row 11.

4. Click on the **ChartWizard button**. It should be the sixth button from the right on your toolbar. If you are using Excel at work or someone has used Excel on your computer before you, it's possible that the Chart-Wizard tool is in another location on the toolbar.

Notice that the cells you highlighted in step 3 are surrounded by a moving border of running ants.

5. Place the **pointer** in cell **A13**. (*Don't click yet.*) The pointer will become a plus sign and a tiny column chart. Line up the plus sign with the top left border of the cell.

6. Press and hold the mouse button as you **drag** the **pointer** diagonally down to **H27**. (This process tells Excel where to place your chart.) Don't be concerned that you cannot see row 27 at first. As you drag the cursor down, the screen will automatically show more rows.

7. When cells A13 through H27 have been enclosed in the border, **release** the mouse button. The ChartWizard – Step 1 of 5 dialog box may appear in a different location from what you see in the next example.

Notice that the Range text box refers to the cells you highlighted in step 3. If the range is not correct, you can type the correct cell reference now. The correct cell range is $A$5:$D$9. This means that you have highlighted the range of cells A5 through D9.

8. **Click** on **Next**. The ChartWizard – Step 2 of 5 dialog box will appear.

Selecting a Column Chart

Notice the 15 different charts you can create with this dialog box.

1. Click on the **Column chart tool** if it is not already highlighted. If it is highlighted, go on to step 2.

2. Click on **Next**. The ChartWizard – Step 3 of 5 dialog box will appear.

Selecting the Chart Format

Notice the 10 different column chart formats you can create with this dialog box.

1. Click on the **Standard Column chart button** (selection number 1) if it is not already highlighted. If it is highlighted, go on to step 2.

2. Click on **Next**. The ChartWizard – Step 4 of 5 dialog box will appear.

Adding a Chart Title

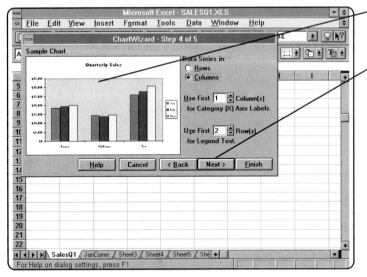

Notice the Sample Chart Preview window.

1. Click on **Next**. The ChartWizard – Step 5 of 5 dialog box will appear.

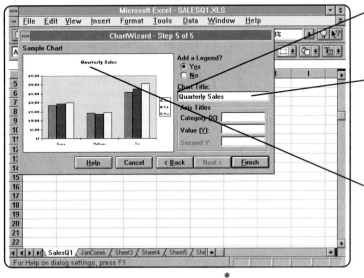

2. Click on the **Chart Title text box** to set the cursor in the box.

3. Type Quarterly Sales. *Do not press Enter or click on Finish until you have completed steps 1 through 5 in the following section.*

Notice that after a brief pause the title "Quarterly Sales" is added to the Sample Chart preview window.

Adding Category and Value Titles

In Excel, X and Y axes titled are called *Category titles* (X axis) and *Value titles* (Y axis). You will add the label "Top Three" to the X axis where the names of the salespeople appear and add "Dollars" to explain that the numbers on the Y-axis scale represent money.

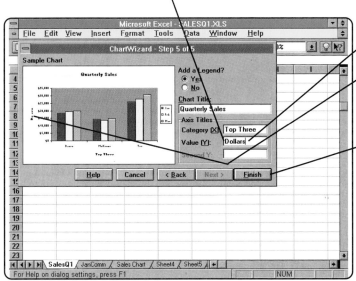

1. **Click** on the **Category (X) text box** to set the cursor in the box.

2. **Type Top Three**. *Do not press Enter or click on Finish.*

After a brief pause, Top Three will appear under the chart.

3. **Click** on the **Value (Y) text box** to set the cursor in the box.

4. **Type Dollars**.

Notice that after a brief pause "Dollars" will appear on the left side of the chart.

5. **Click** on **Finish**. The Quarterly Sales report column chart will appear on your worksheet.

Congratulations! You have created an embedded column chart.

Note: An embedded chart is a permanent part of your worksheet. Whenever you make a change in your worksheet data, the change is reflected in this chart.

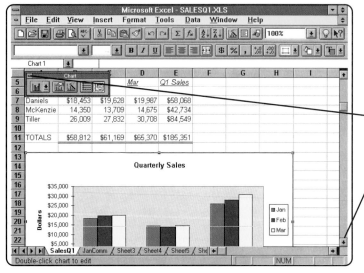

CHANGING THE VIEW

1. **Click twice** on the **Control menu box** on the Chart toolbar to close it.

2. **Click repeatedly** on the ⬇ on the scroll bar to bring the entire chart into view.

MAKING A 3-D COLUMN CHART

Creating a 3-D chart is a two-step process. First you will select the 3-D chart type and then you will change the 3-D format.

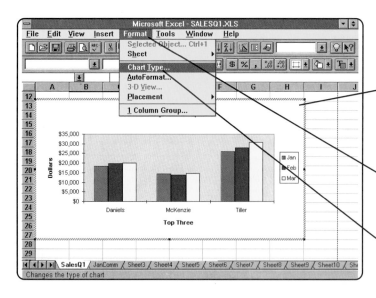

Selecting the Chart Type

1. **Click twice anywhere** on the chart to make it active. The border of the chart will turn into a striped pattern.

2. **Click** on **Format** in the menu bar. A pull-down menu will appear.

3. **Click** on **Chart Type**. The Chart Type dialog box will appear.

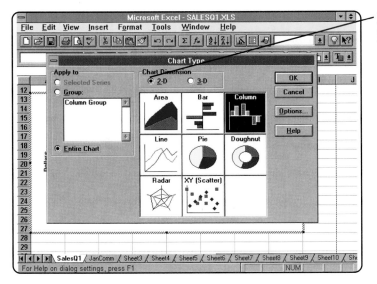

Notice that the 2-D Chart Dimension is selected.

4. Click on **3-D** to place a dot in the circle. Six 3-D chart type options will appear.

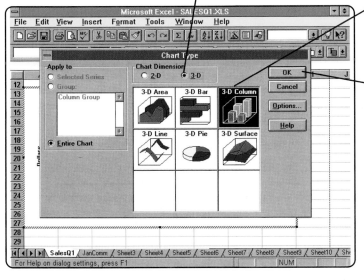

5. Click on the **3-D column chart option** if it is not already highlighted.

6. Click on **OK**. The chart will reappear. Don't panic when you see it. You will quickly fix its weird look in the next section.

Selecting the 3-D Format

Weird, huh?

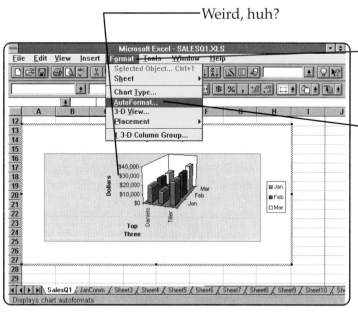

1. Click on **Format** in the menu bar. A pull-down menu will appear.

2. Click on **Auto Format**. The Auto Format dialog box will appear.

Notice that there are eight 3-D column charts and that chart number 5 is highlighted.

3. **Click** on the **first Chart** in the Formats box.

4. **Click** on **OK**. The Quarterly Sales Report chart will now appear in 3-D.

Changing the Colors of the Columns

1. **Click twice** on the **largest Tiller column**. The Format Data Series text box will appear.

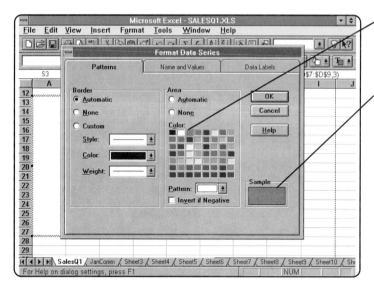

2. Click on the **red square**, the third from the left in the top row of the Color palette.

Notice that the color selected is shown in the Sample box.

3. Click on **OK**. The Quarterly Sales Report chart will appear. The column you selected will now be red.

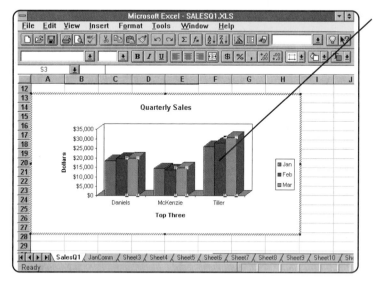

4. Click twice on the middle Tiller column. The Format Data Series text box will appear.

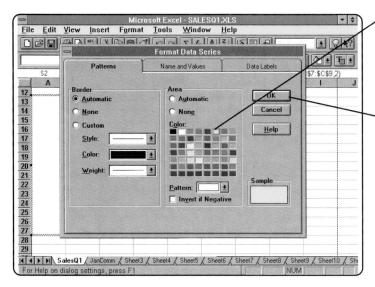

5. **Click** on the **yellow square**, third from the right on the top row of the color palette.

6. **Click** on **OK**. The Quarterly Sales Report chart will appear. The middle column will now become yellow.

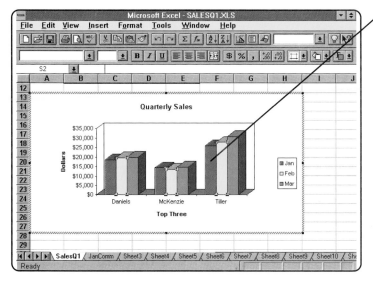

7. **Click twice** on the **shortest Tiller column**. The Format Data Series text box will appear.

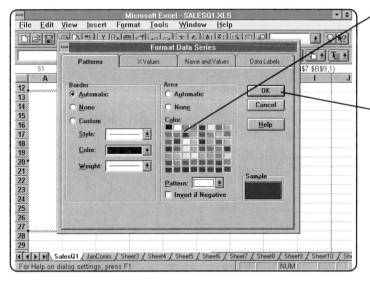

8. Click on the **blue square**, third from the left on the second row of the color palette.

9. Click on **OK**. The Quarterly Sales Report chart will appear. Your chart is now color coordinated!

SAVING THE 3-D BAR CHART

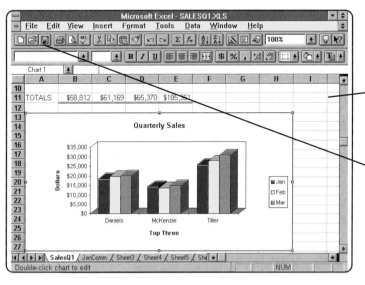

Now that your chart looks like a work of art, you will want to save it.

1. Click anywhere on the **spreadsheet** to turn off the selection of the graph.

2. Click on the **Save button** on the toolbar. Your chart is now saved as part of the SALESQ1 worksheet.

If you plan to follow along to the next chapter, leave the chart on your screen.

Working with Floors and Walls

You can add a lot of pizzazz to a 3-D chart by decorating the walls and floor. You can not only color the walls and floor in a chart, but can also add gridlines to the wall to make it easier to line up the columns with the numbers they represent. In this chapter, you will do the following:

❖ Change the floor color of the chart

❖ Change the wall color of the chart

❖ Add horizontal gridlines using the Chart toolbar

CHANGING THE FLOOR COLOR

1. Open the **SALESQ1 worksheet** if it is not already on your screen.

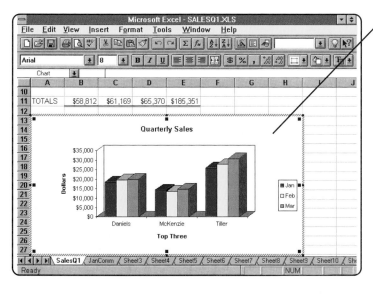

2. Click twice on the white space on the **chart** to select it. The border of the chart will become a striped pattern.

3. **Click twice anywhere** on the **floor** of the chart (the gray, shaded area). The Format Floor dialog box will appear.

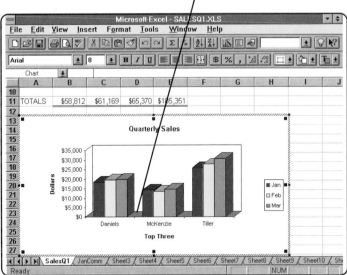

4. **Click** on the **magenta square**, the second from the right in the top row of the palette. Notice that the color will appear in the Sample box.

5. **Click** on **OK**. The Quarterly Sales Report chart will reappear.

CHANGING THE WALL COLOR

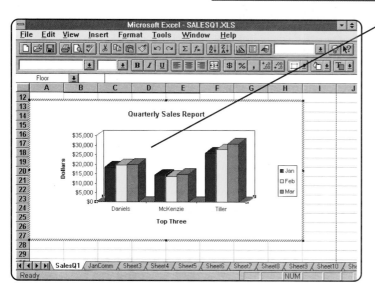

1. **Click twice anywhere** on the **back wall** of the SALESQ1 chart. The Format Walls dialog box will appear.

2. **Click** on the **blue square**, the fourth from the left in the fourth row.

3. **Click** on **OK**. The Quarterly Sales Report chart will reappear with a new color added to the chart.

ADDING GRIDLINES WITH THE CHART TOOLBAR

The easiest way to add gridlines to a chart is to use the Chart toolbar, which you closed in Chapter 17, to improve the view. In this section, you will open the chart toolbar and add gridlines.

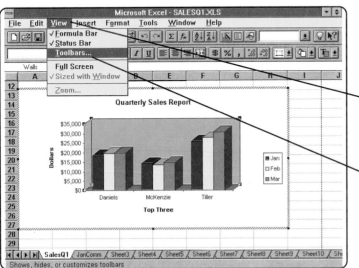

1. Click on **View** in the menu bar. A pull-down menu will appear.

2. Click on **Toolbars**. The Toolbars dialog box will appear.

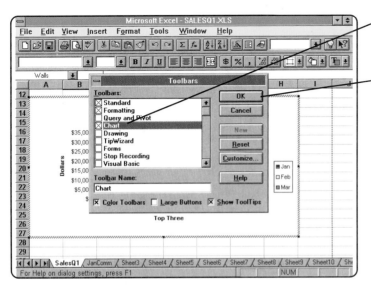

3. Click on **Chart** to place an X in the Box.

4. Click on **OK**. Quarterly Sales Report chart will reappear with the chart toolbar.

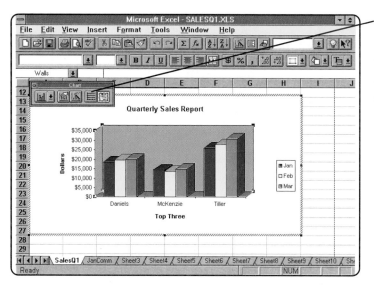

5. **Click** on the **Horizontal Gridlines button** on the toolbar. Gridlines will be added to the walls of the chart.

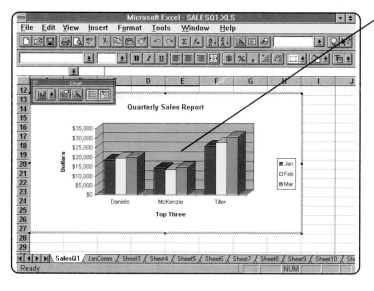

Now notice how much easier it is to read the chart with gridlines.

SAVING THE CHART

1. **Click** on the **Save button** on the toolbar. The chart is now saved with the newly added colors and gridlines.

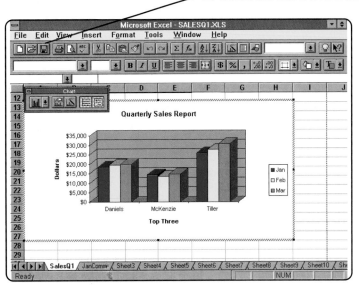

If you plan to follow along to the next chapter, leave the chart on your screen.

Working with Legends and Axis Text

A legend on a map tells you what the symbols on the map mean. Similarly, a chart legend tells you the meaning of the various colors (or shades of gray) of the chart columns. Axis text are the labels on either the X or Y axis. The horizontal axis (X axis) text in the example lists the salespeople's names. The vertical axis (Y axis) shows the amount of sales in dollars. In this chapter, you will do the following:

❖ Change the Y-axis text alignment
❖ Change the Y-axis text
❖ Change the legend format
❖ Delete and restore a legend
❖ Move a legend
❖ Close the chart toolbar

CHANGING THE Y-AXIS TEXT ALIGNMENT

In this section, you will change the alignment of the Y-axis text to horizontal.

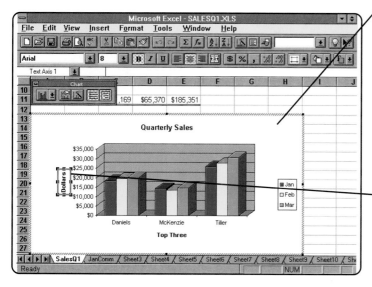

1. **Open** the **SALESQ1 worksheet** if it is not already on your screen.

2. **Click twice** on the white area of the **chart** to select the chart, if it isn't already selected. The border will be surrounded by a striped pattern.

3. **Click** once on **Dollars**. Dollars will be surrounded by a box with small, black handles to indicate that it has been selected.

4. Click on **Format** in the menu bar. A pull-down menu will appear.

5. Click on **Selected Axis Title**. The Format Axis Title dialog box will appear.

6. Click on **Alignment**. The Alignment tab dialog box will appear.

7. Click on **Text** (the horizontal box).

8. Click on **OK**. The Quarterly Sales chart will appear.

Notice that the text, "Dollars," is now aligned horizontally.

CHANGING THE Y-AXIS TEXT

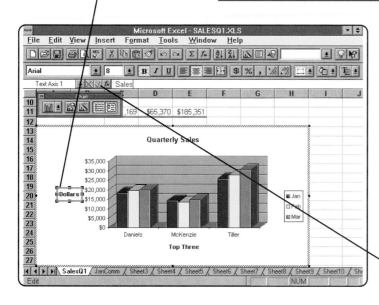

In this section, you will replace the Y-axis text "Dollars" with the text "Sales."

1. Move the mouse **pointer** up to the **contents box**. The pointer will change to an I-beam.

2. Click once to set the cursor and **type Sales**.

3. Click on ✔ or press **Enter**. The Quarterly Sales chart will reappear.

Notice that the text "Dollars" has been replaced by the text "Sales."

CHANGING THE LEGEND FORMAT

1. **Click twice anywhere** on the **Legend box**. The legend box will be surrounded with small, black handles. The Format legend dialog box appears.

2. **Click** on the **Font tab**. The Font dialog box will appear.

Notice that you can view the list of fonts that are available by clicking on the ⬇ on the scroll bar.

3. **Click** on **Bold** to change the font style. Bold will appear in the Font style box.

4. **Click** on **10** to change the point size. Ten (10) will appear in the size box.

5. **Click** on **OK**. The Quarterly Sales chart will appear. The legend text will now be 10-point Arial Bold.

DELETING AND RESTORING A LEGEND

To delete and restore a legend, it is not necessary to have the legend selected.

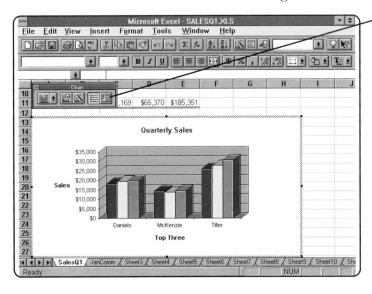

1. Click on the **Legend button** on the toolbar. The legend will be deleted from the chart.

2. Click again on the **Legend button** on the toolbar. The legend will be restored to the chart.

Notice that when the legend is restored, it does not retain the 10-point bold formatting created previously in "Changing the Legend Format."

MOVING THE LEGEND

In this section, you will move the legend to the lower left corner of the chart.

1. Click on the **legend** if it does not alredy have selection handles.

2. Press and hold the mouse button as you **drag** down to the **bottom** of the **chart**. A dotted frame will move as you drag.

3. Continue holding the mouse button and **drag** the dotted **frame** to the **left corner** of the chart.

4. Release the **mouse button** when the dotted frame for the legend is placed in the left corner of the chart. The legend text will move to the left corner.

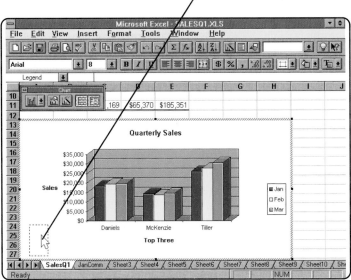

CLOSING THE CHART TOOLBAR

Notice that the legend appears in the exact location where you placed the dotted frame.

1. Click once on the **Control menu box** on the Chart toolbar. The toolbar will close.

SAVING THE CHART

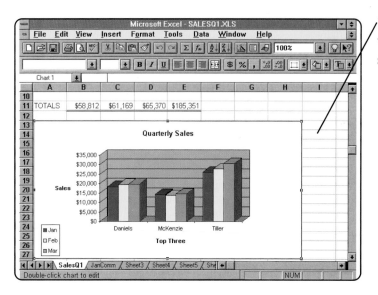

1. **Click anywhere** on the **worksheet** to remove the striped border.

2. **Click** on the **Save button** on the toolbar. The Quarterly Sales chart and the worksheet are now saved with the new formatting.

If you plan to follow along with the next chapter, leave the chart on your screen.

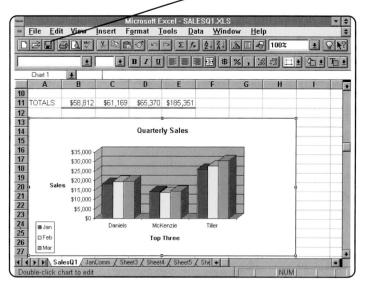

Adding Chart Text, Shapes, and Arrows

Customizing a chart in Excel 5 is a snap. As you saw in the examples in the previous chapter, you can move a chart text box anywhere on the chart by simply clicking on the text box and dragging it to another location. You also saw that you can style text and change text alignment with the Format menu. As you will see in this chapter, you can add additional text boxes (in addition to those automatically created by Excel) and put them anywhere on the chart. Moreover, you can draw arrows and other shapes and place them anywhere on the chart. In this chapter, you will do the following:

❖ Add text to the chart and draw an oval around the text

❖ Color an oval

❖ Add an arrow

ADDING TEXT

1. Open the **SALESQ1** worksheet if it isn't already on your screen.

2. Click twice on the **chart**. It will be surrounded by a striped border.

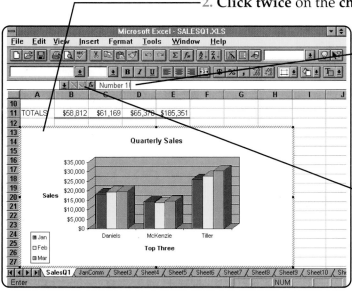

3. Type Number 1! (Be sure to include the exclamation point.) As you begin to type, the letters will show up in the formula bar. The Cancel box (✗) and the Enter box (✔) will appear.

4. Click on ✔ or **press Enter**. The text will appear on the chart surrounded by black handles.

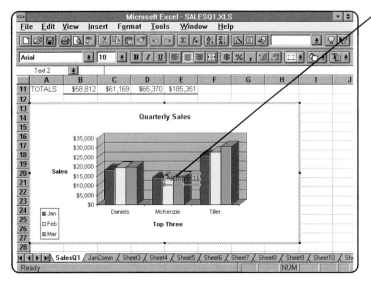

Notice that the text box mysteriously placed itself in this location. Your text box may end up in a different place. The next step is to move it to a different location.

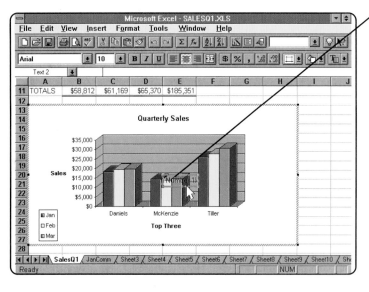

5. Place the **mouse pointer** on the **border** of the text box. Do not place it on one of the handles on the inside of the box.

6. Press and hold the mouse button. When you begin to drag in the next step, a dotted box will appear.

7. While pressing and holding the mouse button, **drag** the **dotted box** to a place on the chart where you want the "Number 1!" text to appear. The "Number 1!" text will not move until you release the mouse button. **Note:** In the next section, you will draw an oval (ellipse) around the text. In the section following it, you will draw an arrow from the text to Tiller's highest column. Place the text so that there is room for the oval and arrow.

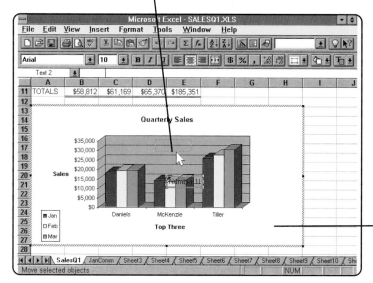

8. Release the mouse button. The text will move to the new location.

9. Click on **any blank spot** on the **chart**. The black handles will disappear.

DRAWING AN OVAL AROUND THE TEXT

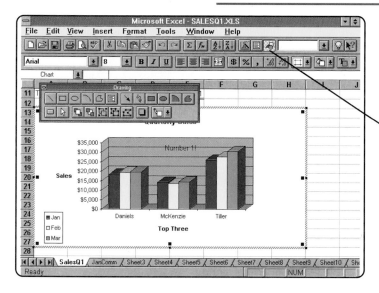

In this section, you will draw an oval (ellipse) around the text, "Number 1!"

1. Click on the **Draw button** on the toolbar. The Drawing toolbar will appear.

2. Click on the **Ellipse button** on the Drawing toolbar. The button will become recessed. The cursor will become a crosshair.

3. Move the **crosshair** to the **left** of the **text** where you want to begin drawing the oval (ellipse).

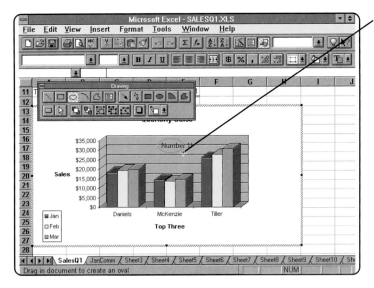

4. Press and hold the mouse button as you **drag** the **crosshair down** and to the **right**.

Notice that an oval will form as you drag the crosshair. The idea is to surround "Number 1!" with the oval.

5. **Release** the mouse button. The text will be surrounded by an oval. The oval itself will be surrounded by square handles.

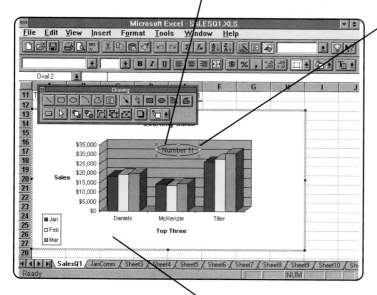

To change the size and shape of the oval, put your mouse pointer on any handle. The pointer will change to a two-headed arrow. **Press and hold** the mouse button as you **drag** the **handle**. Drag toward the middle of the oval to make the oval smaller. Drag out to make it larger. You may have to fiddle with it to get it to look the way you want.

6. **Click once anywhere** on a white area of the **chart**. The black handles will disappear. "Number 1!" will be surrounded by an oval.

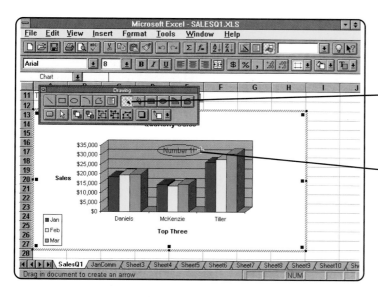

ADDING AN ARROW

1. **Click** on the **Arrow button**. The cursor will turn into a black crosshair.

2. **Place** the **crosshair** on the **right edge** of the **oval**.

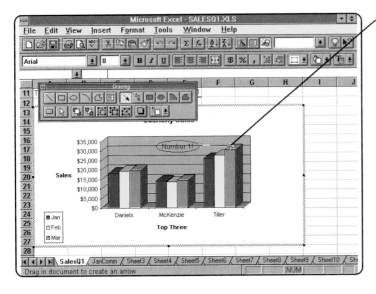

3. Press and hold the mouse button as you **drag** the **crosshair** toward the **highest column** in the Tiller area. The arrow line that appears as you drag will look jagged. It will print straight, though.

4. Release the mouse button. An arrowhead will be added to the arrow line.

COLORING THE OVAL

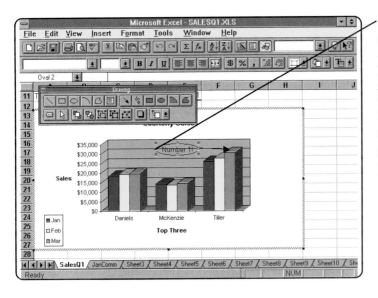

1. Click on the **edge** of the **oval**. (You have to be very precise about where you place the mouse arrow before you click or else you may click on the text box by accident). The oval will be surrounded by square handles.

2. **Click** on **Format** in the menu bar. A pull-down menu will appear.

3. **Click** on **Selected Object**. The Format Object dialog box will appear.

4. **Click** on the **yellow square**, the third from the right in the top row.

5. **Click** on **OK**. The chart will reappear with a yellow background in the oval. FANTASTIC!

If the yellow covers your text, click on the Send to Back tool on the Draw tool-bar. It is the fourth tool from the left in the second row.

If you plan to go on to the next chapter, don't close the Drawing toolbar. Go on to the section after next, "Saving the Chart."

CLOSING THE DRAWING TOOLBAR

1. Click once on the **Control menu box** (⊟) on the left side of the Drawing title bar. The drawing toolbar will disappear.

2. Click once **anywhere off** the **chart**. The handles will disappear from around the oval, and the chart will be surrounded by a black border with handles.

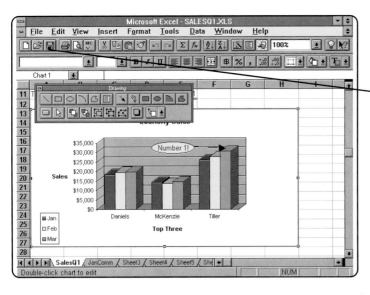

SAVING THE CHART

1. Click on the **Save button**.

Isn't this great? You now have a terrific-looking 3-D column chart. If you want to get even more sophisticated, complete the next two chapters!

Grouping and Moving Graphics

If you've worked with graphics and text boxes before, you know how frustrating it can be to move them around one at a time when you want to place them somewhere else on your chart. Excel 5 makes this an easy task by allowing you to group several objects together and move them as a unit. In this chapter, you will do the following:

❖ Group together an oval, text box, and arrow

❖ Move the group to a new location

❖ Close the drawing toolbar

❖ Save the chart

GROUPING AN OVAL, TEXT BOX, AND ARROW

In this section, you will make several graphic elements into a group by drawing a "lasso" around them.

1. **Open** the **Drawing toolbar** if it is not already open. If you need help opening the Drawing toolbar, see Chapter 20, the section entitled "Drawing an Oval Around the Text."

2. **Click twice** in the white area of the **chart**. It will be surrounded by a striped border.

3. **Click** on the **white arrow** on the Drawing toolbar. It will become recessed.

4. **Place** the **mouse arrow** above and to the left of the **oval**. When you press the mouse button, the arrow will become a crosshair.

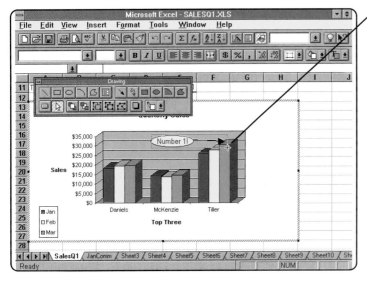

5. **Press and hold** the mouse button as you **drag** the crosshair **down and** to the **right**. Make sure you get the entire arrow inside the lasso. The oval, the text box, and the arrow will become surrounded by a dotted, rectangular frame.

6. **Release** the mouse button. The oval, text box, and arrow are now "grouped together" and all are surrounded by handles. If *all* of the elements are not surrounded by handles, it means you did not place the crosshair far enough outside the oval so that the entire oval was inside the lasso.

MOVING THE GROUPED TEXT AND GRAPHICS

1. **Place** the mouse arrow **anywhere** on the **oval**.

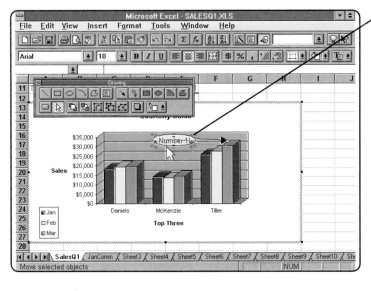

2. **Press and hold** the mouse button as you **move** the **group** to another location to better line it up. You may have to fiddle with this to improve the "look." Neat!

3. **Click** once **anywhere** on the worksheet to remove the border.

CLOSING THE DRAWING TOOLBAR

1. Click on the **Control menu box** (⊟) on the left side of the Drawing title bar. The drawing toolbar will disappear.

SAVING THE CHART

1. Click on the **Save button**.

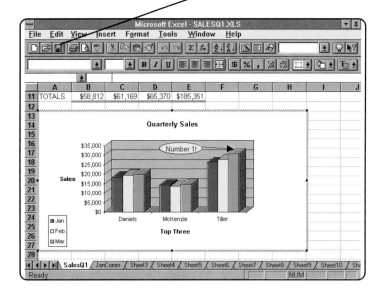

If you plan to follow along to the next chapter, leave the chart on the screen.

Styling a Chart

In Excel, there are many ways you can make your chart more attractive. You can change the text fonts, background color, and patterns and even add colored borders around text blocks. You are limited only by your imagination! If you are printing in black and white, the Patterns option improves a chart's appearance when you print. In this chapter, you will do the following:

❖ Add a colored border and shadow to a text box

❖ Change the font in a text box

❖ Add a colored border around the chart area

❖ Add and remove patterns on the columns

ADDING A COLORED BORDER AND SHADOW

In this section, you will add a colored border with a shadow to the chart title text box.

1. Click twice anywhere on the **chart** if it is not surrounded by a striped border.

2. Click twice on the chart title, **Quarterly Sales**. The format Title dialog box will appear. If it doesn't, click on several different items on the chart and then click off the chart and start again.

3. Click on **Custom** in the Border area to place a dot in the circle.

4. Click on the ⬇ to the right of color. A drop-down Color palette will appear.

5. Click on the **blue square** in the top row, the fifth square from the left. The blue color will appear in the sample color box.

6. Click on the ⬇ to the right of the Weight box. A drop-down list of border options will appear.

7. Click on the **border option** shown here. It will appear in the Weight box, and the sample border will show in the Sample box.

8. **Click** on **Shadow** to put an ✕ in the box. The Sample box will now show the shadow.

9. **Click** on **OK**. The Quarterly Sales chart will reappear.

10. **Click anywhere** on the white section of the chart. The selection handles will disappear.

CHANGING THE FONT IN A TEXT BOX

In this example, you will change the font in the Number 1 text box to bold.

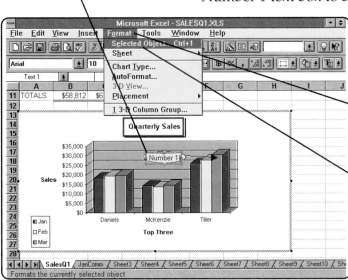

1. **Click** on **Number 1!** The text box will be surrounded by a border with handles.

2. **Click** on **Format** in the menu bar. A pull-down menu will appear.

3. **Click** on **Selected Object**. The Format Object dialog box will appear.

4. Click on the **Font tab**. The Font Format dialog box will appear.

5. Click on **Bold**. Bold will become highlighted and the word Bold will appear in the font style box.

6. Click on **OK**. The chart will appear.

7. Click anywhere on the **white surface** of the chart. The selection handles will disappear.

ADDING A BORDER TO A CHART

In this section, you will add a red border to surround the chart area.

Notice the blue border and shadow.

Notice the bold font.

1. Click anywhere on the **white surface** of the chart. Handles will appear just inside the striped border.

2. Click on **Format** in the menu bar. A pull-down menu will appear.

3. Click on **Selected Chart Area**. The Format Chart Area dialog box will appear.

4. Click on **Patterns**. The Patterns dialog box will appear.

5. Click on **Custom** to place a dot in the circle.

6. Click on the ⬇ in the color text box. A drop-down color palette will appear.

7. Click on the **red square**, the third square from the left in the top row. The red square will appear in the sample color box.

8. Click on the ⬇ to the right of the Weight box. A drop-down list of border weights will appear.

9. Click on the **border** at the bottom of the list. It will appear in the Weight box.

10. Click on **OK**. The chart will appear surrounded by a red border.

ADDING A PATTERN TO A CHART COLUMN

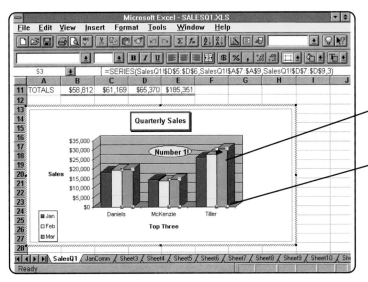

In this section, you will add a pattern to the March column for the three sales executives.

1. Click on **Tiller's March column**.

Notice that the white handles appear on the March columns of the three salespeople.

2. Click on **Format** in the menu bar. A pull-down menu will appear.

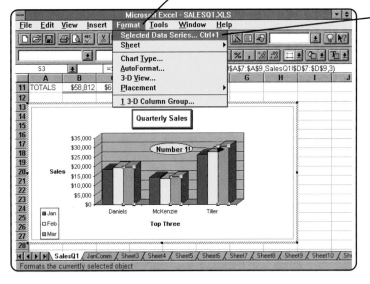

3. Click on **Selected Series**. The Format Data Series dialog box will appear.

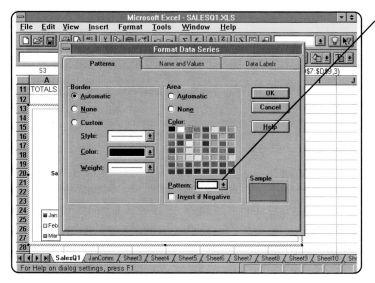

4. Click on the ⬇ to the right of Pattern. A pop-up pattern palette will appear.

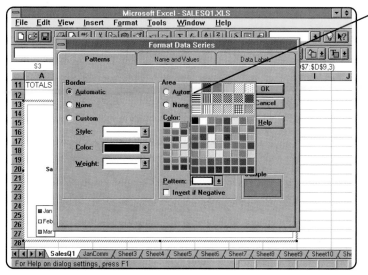

5. Click on the **pattern** on the far left side of the second row from the top. The pattern will appear in the Sample box.

Notice the pattern in the Sample box.

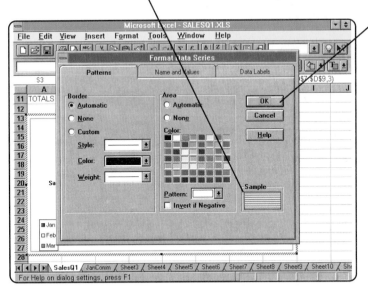

6. Click on **OK**. The chart will reappear with the striped pattern you selected for the March columns.

Note: You can repeat steps 1 through 6 to put different patterns on the Jan and Feb columns.

REMOVING THE PATTERNS

Make certain that the columns from which you want to remove the patterns are selected.

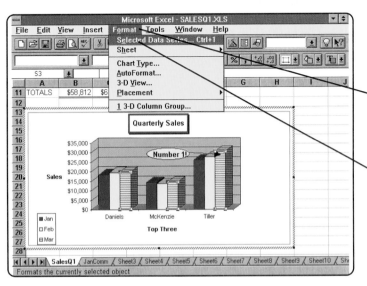

Note: The March columns should be selected with white handles.

1. Click on **Format** on the menu bar. A pull-down menu will appear.

2. Click on **Selected Data Series**. The Format Data Series dialog box will appear.

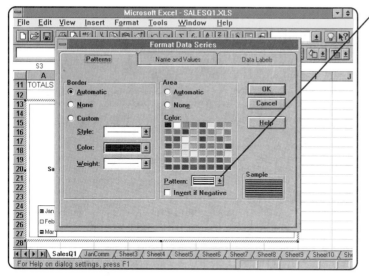

3. Click on the ⬇ to the right of the Pattern text box. A pop-up pattern palette will appear.

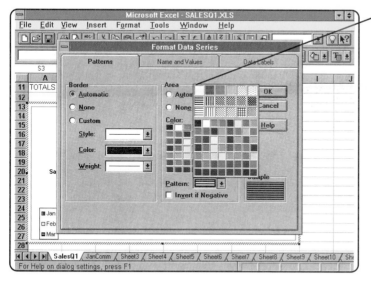

4. Click on the **white square** in the top left corner of the pattern palette. The pop-up palette will disappear. The Pattern box will be white, and the Sample box will be solid red.

5. **Click** on **OK**. Voilà! The column is now solid red!

6. **Click once** off the chart area. The chart will be surrounded by the red border. The selection handles and striped border will disappear.

SAVING THE STYLE

1. **Click** on the **Save button** on the toolbar.

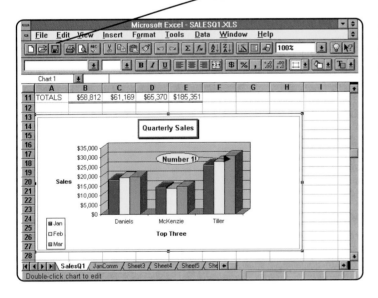

If you plan to follow along to the next chapter, leave the chart on your screen.

Copying and Printing Charts

In Excel 5, you can put a chart on a different sheet within the workbook file. This makes it easy to print the chart without the worksheet data. The chart remains linked to the original worksheet data, however, so that any changes you make in the worksheet are reflected in the chart. If you leave the chart in the worksheet where you created it, you can print both the chart and worksheet data together. In this chapter, you will do the following:

❖ Copy a chart to a separate sheet within the workbook

❖ Print a chart

❖ Print a chart and a worksheet on the same page

❖ Preview and print a chart and a worksheet sideways (in landscape orientation)

COPYING THE CHART TO ANOTHER SHEET

In this section, you will copy a chart to another sheet and save it.

1. **Click twice** on the white area of the **chart**. It will become surrounded by a striped border with handles.

2. Click on the **Copy button** in the toolbar. The chart will be surrounded by a border of running ants.

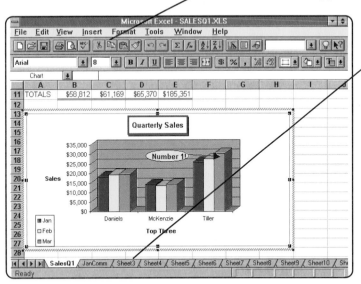

3. Click on the **Sheet 3 tab**. An empty worksheet will appear.

4. Click on the **Paste button** on the toolbar. A copy of the chart will appear on the sheet.

Note: When you click on the Paste button, the chart that is copied to the worksheet remains linked to the original embedded chart. When you make a change in the data in the SALESQ1.XLS worksheet, therefore, the changes will be reflected in this chart.

If you do not want to link the chart, you can click on Edit in the menu bar and click on Paste Special and then on Picture. The chart you copy this way can be sized proportionally like a graphic and will not be linked to the data in the SALESQ1.XLS worksheet.

PRINTING THE CHART

1. Click on the **Print button** on the toolbar. A printing message box will appear briefly. After a short intermission, the chart will print.

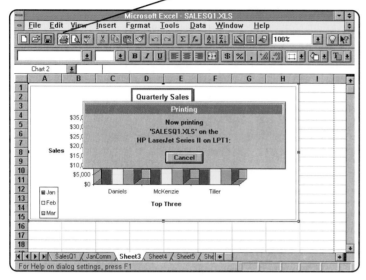

NAMING AND SAVING THE SHEET

1. Click twice on **Sheet3**. The Rename Sheet dialog box will appear.

2. Type Sales Chart.

3. Click on **OK**. The rename Sheet dialog box will appear.

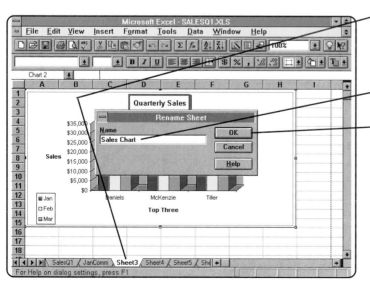

4. **Click** on the **Save button** on the toolbar. A copy of the Quarterly Sales chart is now saved to a new sheet.

Notice the new name for the tab.

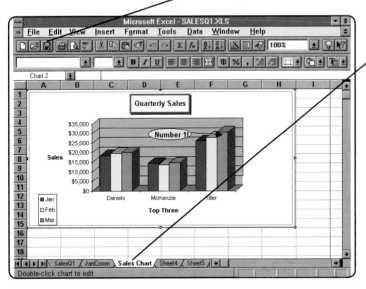

PRINTING A WORKSHEET AND A CHART AT THE SAME TIME

1. **Click** on the **SALESQ1 tab**. The first worksheet and chart will appear.

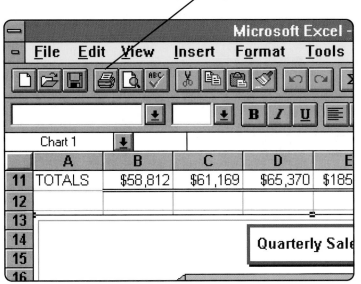

2. Click on the **Print button** in the toolbar. The Printing message box will appear. The SALESQ1.XLS worksheet and chart will be printed together on the same page.

3. If you change your mind, **click** on **Cancel** in the Printing message box.

PRINTING A WORKSHEET AND CHART SIDEWAYS

There may be a time when you will want to print both a worksheet and a chart sideways (in *landscape* orientation) on your paper, especially if your worksheet is quite wide.

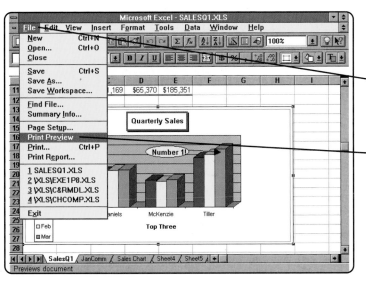

1. Click on **File** in the menu bar. A pull-down menu will appear.

2. Click on **Print Preview**. The Print Preview screen will appear.

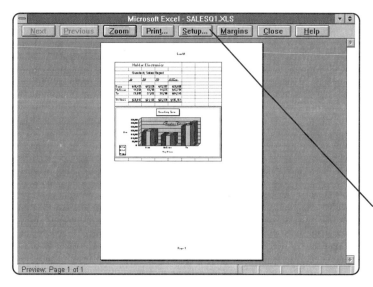

Most documents are normally printed in portrait orientation, with the short side of the paper at the top. This is what you will see the first time you select the Print Preview option. This preview is an example of a portrait orientation.

3. **Click** on **Setup**. The Page Setup dialog box will appear.

Landscape printing means printing with the long side of the paper on top. Landscape printing is often used to print financial worksheets and charts that are too wide to be printed in portrait.

4. **Click** on **Landscape** in the Orientation option box to place a dot inside the circle.

5. **Click** on **OK**. The worksheet and chart will appear in landscape orientation in the print preview screen.

6. Click on **Print**. The Print Preview screen will disappear. The Print dialog box will appear.

7. Click on **OK**. The Printing message box will appear briefly. The worksheet and chart will be printed sideways.

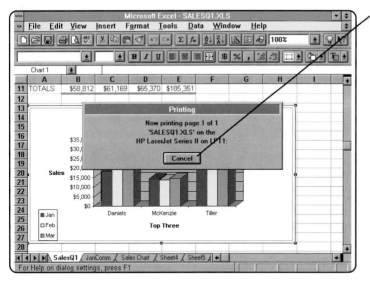

If you want to cancel the printing job, **click** on **Cancel**.

Switching Back to Portrait Printing

It is a good idea to switch back to portrait printing at this time. Otherwise, the next time you print something it will be printed sideways.

1. **Click** on **File** in the menu bar. A pull-down menu will appear.

2. **Click** on **Print Preview**. The Print Preview screen will appear. The preview window will show the worksheet in landscape orientation.

3. **Click** on **Setup**. The Page Setup dialog box will reappear.

4. **Click** on **Portrait** in the Orientation option box to place a dot inside the circle.

5. **Click** on **OK**. The Print Preview screen will show the worksheet in portrait orientation.

Your printer will now print in portrait mode.

6. **Click** on **Close**. The Quarterly Sales Report chart will appear.

If you are going on to Chapter 24, you need not exit or save at this time.

Program Manager

Part V: Special Features

Dynamic
Data Exchange

Another terrific feature of Windows is that you can link a worksheet chart into a word-processed document. When a worksheet chart is linked to a word-processed document, *any changes made in the worksheet chart are automatically reflected* in the document. This feature is called *Dynamic Data Exchange*. In this chapter, you will do the following:

❖ Copy a chart to the Windows Clipboard

❖ Open a Windows Write document file

❖ Paste-link a chart to a Windows Write document

❖ Observe the link in action

THE COPY-AND-LINK PROCESS

The copy-and-link process described in this chapter consists of four stages:

Stage 1: Copy the Excel chart to the windows Clipboard

Stage 2: Keep Excel running in the background

Stage 3: Open a word-processed document into which you will paste-link the chart

Stage 4: Paste-link a copy of the Excel chart from the clipboard into the word-processed document

Copying a Chart to the Windows Clipboard

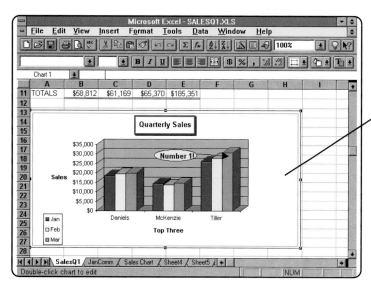

1. **Open** the **SALESQ1** worksheet containing the Quarterly Sales Report you created in Part IV.

2. **Click** in the white area of the chart to select it. The chart will be surrounded by a border with handles. Make sure that the striped border is not selected. If it is, click once anywhere on the worksheet and try again.

3. **Click** on **Edit** in the menu bar. A pull-down menu will appear.

4. **Click** on **Copy**. The chart will be copied to the Clipboard. The chart is now ready to be linked to a word-processed document file.

Running Excel in the Background

To link the Quarterly Sales Report chart to a word-processed document, Excel must be running in the background.

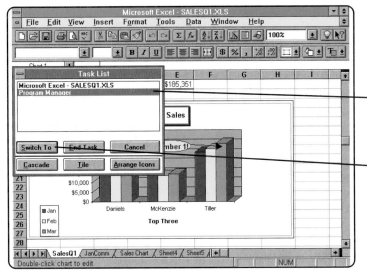

1. **Press and hold** the **Ctrl key** and **press** the **Esc key** (Ctrl + Esc). The Task List dialog box will appear.

2. **Click** on **Program Manager**. It will become highlighted.

3. **Click** on **Switch To**. The Program Manager windows will appear in the foreground. The Excel window will move to the background.

Opening a Word-Processed Document

We used Windows Write as the word-processing program in this example. However, Word, WordPerfect for Windows and Ami Pro all link charts in much the same way.

1. **Click twice** on the **icon** of the word-processing program you use.

Linking the Chart

This example shows a maximized screen with the chart being linked to a memo that was written in Write. However, you can link into a blank document file if you don't want to bother typing the memo text.

1. **Move** the **cursor** to the spot on the document where you want to paste-link the copy of the Quarterly Sales chart.

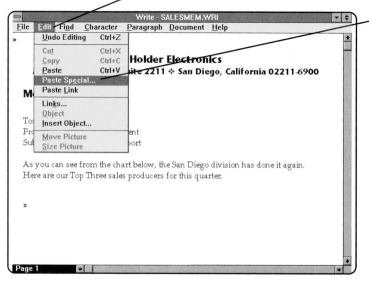

2. **Click** on **Edit** in the menu bar. A pull-down menu will appear.

3. **Click** on **Paste Special**. The Paste Special dialog box will appear.

4. Click on **Picture** in the Data Type dialog box. (We recommend that you choose Picture because the file size will be smaller and take up less space on your drive than if you choose Microsoft Excel 5.0 Chart Object.)

5. Click on **Paste Link**. The Quarterly Sales chart will appear in the word-processed document.

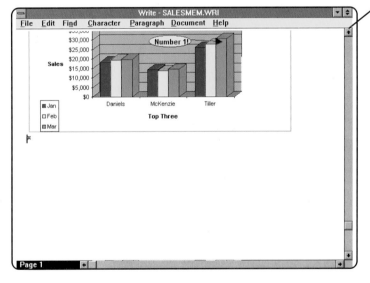

6. Click repeatedly on the ↑ on the scroll bar to bring the chart into view.

CENTERING THE CHART IN THE WORD-PROCESSED DOCUMENT

1. Click on the **chart** to select it. In Write, it will appear with black highlighting. It may not have black highlighting in other word-processing programs.

2. Click on **Paragraph** in the menu bar. A pull-down menu will appear.

3. Click on **Centered**. The chart will move to the center of the page.

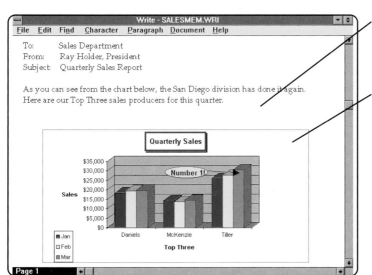

4. Click once anywhere on the memo. The chart will no longer appear highlighted.

Notice that the chart is now centered in the memo.

VIEWING EXCEL AND WRITE SIDE BY SIDE

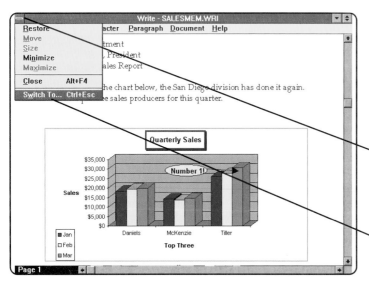

To really appreciate how a link works, you must see it in action. In this section, you will place the Excel worksheet and the word-processed memo side by side (called *tiling*).

1. Click on the **Control menu box** (⊟) on the left side of the title bar. A pull-down menu will appear.

2. Click on **Switch To**. The Task List dialog box will appear.

Caution: To place (tile) two programs side by side, no other programs can be running except Program Manager, which must be minimized. If your Task List shows programs other than the three listed in this example, close them before proceeding.

Exception: If you have ATM or Print Cache 3.1 running, they may show up on your Task List, but they do not need to be closed.

3. Click on **Program Manager**.

4. Click on **Switch To**. The Program Manager window will appear.

5. **Click** on the **Minimize button** (▼) to the right of the Program Manager title bar. The Program Manager screen will disappear. The Write Document window will move to the foreground.

6. **Click** on the **Control menu box** (▭) to the left of the Write title bar. A pull-down menu will appear.

7. **Click** on **Switch To**. The Task List dialog box will appear.

8. **Click** on **Microsoft Excel**.

9. **Click** on **Tile**. The two windows. Write and Excel, will appear side by side.

Enlarging the Two Windows

To get a better view, you must enlarge both windows.

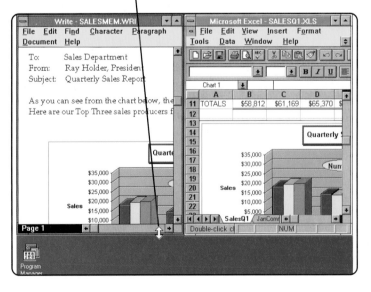

1. **Place** the **pointer** on the **bottom edge** of the **Write window**. The pointer will turn into a two-headed arrow.

2. **Press and hold** the mouse button as you **drag** the **edge** of the window to the **bottom** of the screen. As you drag, the border of the window will expand. It's okay to cover the Program Manager icon.

3. **Release** the mouse button. The Write window will expand to the bottom of the screen.

4. **Repeat steps 1 through 3** to enlarge the Excel window.

5. **Click repeatedly** on the **scroll bar arrows** on *both windows* until your view approximates the one in this example. You want to be able to see the Daniels columns on the chart in the word-processing window and, at the same time, see the worksheet sales figures in the Excel window. You may have to fiddle with the two scroll bars in each window to get there.

TESTING THE LINK

1. **Click anywhere** on the Excel worksheet to make it the active window.

2. **Click twice** on **B7** on the worksheet to open it for in-cell editing. The current sales numbers for this cell will appear in the contents box.

3. Click twice in **B7** to highlight the contents of the cell.

4. Type 60000.

5. Press the **Enter key** and watch the fun. Daniels' January column will automatically enlarge in both windows. The link works!

6. Click on the **Undo button** in the toolbar to undo the change. The worksheet and the linked chart will return to their original versions.

Just for Fun!

Try changing other numbers on the worksheet and watch the resulting changes in the word-processing document chart.

If you are going to use the Excel worksheet to complete other chapters in this book, remember to change the numbers on the worksheet back to their original amounts.

MAXIMIZING EXCEL

1. Click on the **Maximize button** (▲) on the right side of the title bar. Excel will become full size.

CLOSING THE WRITE DOCUMENT

1. **Click** on the **Control menu box** (☐) to the left of the Excel title bar. A pull-down menu will appear.

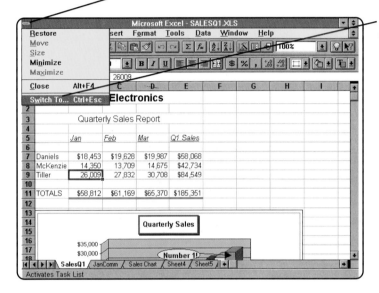

2. **Click** on **Switch To**. The Task List dialog box will appear.

3. **Click** on **Write** or the name of your word-processing program to select it.

4. **Click** on **End Task**. The Write Save Changes dialog box will appear.

5. **Click** on **No**. The Write document will close. The Excel window will reappear.

MAXIMIZING PROGRAM MANAGER

1. **Click** on the **Control menu box** (⊟) on the left side of the Excel title bar. A pull-down menu will appear.

2. **Click** on **Switch To**. The Task List dialog box will appear.

3. **Click** on **Program Manager** to highlight it.

4. **Click** on **Switch To**. The group window will appear.

Notice that Program Manager is now maximized.

RETURNING TO THE EXCEL WORKSHEET

1. **Click** on the **Control menu box** (⊟) on the left side of the menu title bar. A pull-down menu will appear.

2. **Click** on **Switch To**. The Task List dialog box will appear.

3. **Click** on **Microsoft Excel**.

4. **Click** on **Switch to** to return to the program. The Excel SALESQ1 spreadsheet will reappear.

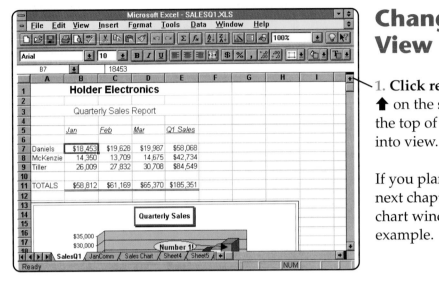

Changing the View

1. **Click repeatedly** on the ⬆ on the scroll bar to bring the top of the worksheet into view.

If you plan to go on to the next chapter now, leave the chart window as it is in this example.

Customizing and Adding Toolbars

In Excel 5, you can change the look of your workplace by removing or adding toolbars from your screen. You can customize one or more of the standard toolbars or create a new toolbar. You can move buttons around from one toolbar to another and put the buttons you use the most on one toolbar. You can place toolbars in various spots on the screen and make the buttons larger. The layout of your workplace is limited only by your own creativity. In this chapter, you will do the following:

❖ Hide a toolbar
❖ Create a new toolbar
❖ Delete selected toolbar buttons
❖ Move selected toolbar buttons to the new toolbar
❖ Make the toolbar buttons larger
❖ Move a toolbar to a different location
❖ Delete the custom toolbar
❖ Restore the original toolbar

HIDING A TOOLBAR

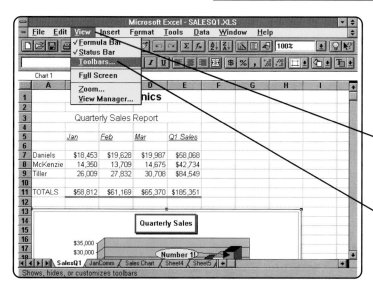

In this section, you will hide the Formatting toolbar.

1. **Open SALESQ1.XLS** if it is not already open.

2. **Click** on **View** in the menu bar. A pull-down menu will appear.

3. **Click** on **Toolbars**. The Toolbars dialog box will appear.

4. Click on **Formatting** to *remove* the X from the box.

5. Click on **OK**. The Formatting toolbar will no longer appear on the desktop screen.

CREATING A NEW TOOLBAR

In this section, you will create a new toolbar. In the sections that follow, you will move selected toolbar buttons to the new toolbar.

1. Place the **mouse arrow anywhere** on the standard toolbar.

2. Click the *right* **mouse button**. A pop-down menu will appear.

3. Click on **Toolbars**. The Toolbar dialog box will appear.

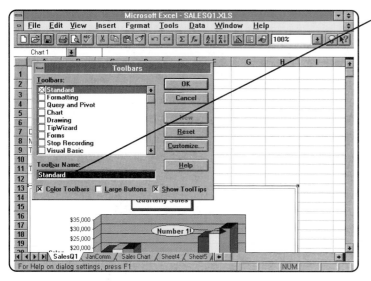

4. Click twice on the word **"Standard"** in the Toolbar Name box. The entire text box will become highlighted.

5. Type My Tools.

6. Click on **Customize**. A tiny toolbar will appear in the upper left corner of the screen. The Customize dialog box will appear. You now have an empty toolbar ready to be filled with your favorite tools!

MOVING A DIALOG BOX

Your dialog box may appear at the top of your screen, as you see in this example. If so, it will not interfere with the steps in the following section, but it will cause your new toolbar to look different from the one you see in these examples. You can move any dialog box very easily.

1. **Place** the mouse arrow on **top** of the dialog box **title bar**.

2. **Press and hold** the mouse button and **drag** the dialog box down **toward** the **bottom** of the screen. You will see an outline of the dialog box being dragged.

3. **Release** the mouse button when the outline is positioned where you want the dialog box to be. The dialog box will move into the new position.

MOVING BUTTONS TO A NEW TOOLBAR

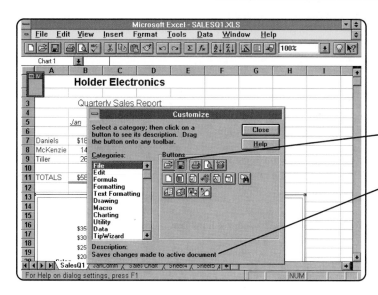

In this section, you will customize the new toolbar with the Save and Print buttons and then add some text formatting buttons.

1. **Click** on the **Save button**. It will become recessed.

Notice that the description of the Save button appears at the bottom of the dialog box.

2. **Click and hold** on the **Save button** and **drag** it **to** the tiny **toolbar** in the corner. You will see an outline of the button being dragged.

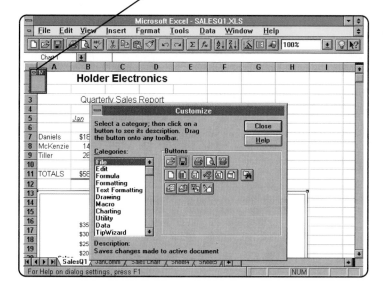

3. **Release** the mouse button. The Save button tool will appear in the new toolbar.

Notice the Save button in the new toolbar.

4. Repeat steps 1 through 3 to place the Print button beside the Save button in the toolbar.

Notice the Print button.

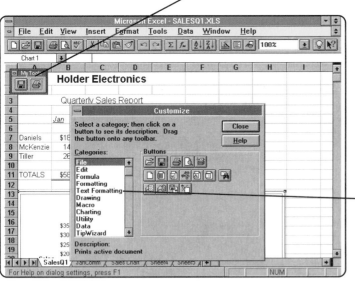

(If, on your screen, the Customize dialog box is to the right of the new My Tools box, the new toolbox will not have room to expand to the right. It will, therefore, expand vertically as you add buttons, instead of horizontally, as you see in this example.)

5. Click on **Text Formatting** to highlight it. The text formatting buttons will appear in the buttons box.

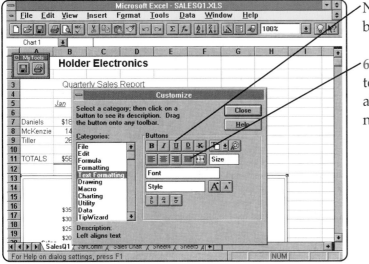

Notice that the selection of button tools has changed.

6. Repeat steps 1 through 3 to put each of the four alignment buttons in the new toolbar.

7. Repeat steps 1 through 3 to place each of the following buttons in the new toolbar:

Bold

Italics

Underline

Font size

Font tool

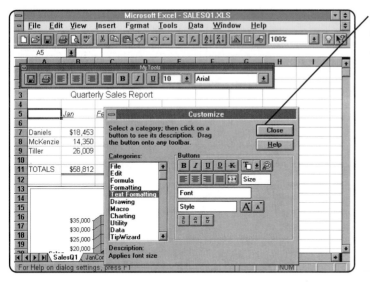

8. Click on **Close**. The worksheet will appear with the new tool showing.

MOVING THE NEW TOOLBAR

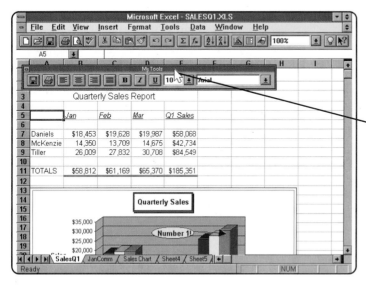

In Excel you can move toolbars to various locations by clicking on the title bar and dragging them. This is called *docking*.

1. Place the **mouse arrow** on the **title bar** of the toolbar.

2. Press and hold the mouse button and **drag** up **toward** the **Standard toolbar**. You will drag an outline of the toolbar. The toolbar itself will not move.

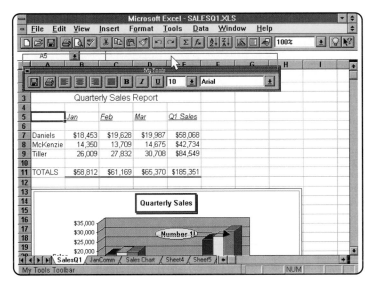

3. **Release** the mouse button when the outline is just below the Standard toolbar. My Tools toolbar will dock itself right under the Standard toolbar. Magic!

DELETING BUTTONS FROM THE STANDARD TOOLBAR

As you work, you may find that there are buttons you don't use very often. You can delete these to make room for other buttons or to make more space for large buttons. In this section, you will delete buttons from the Standard toolbar that are duplicated on the My Tools toolbar.

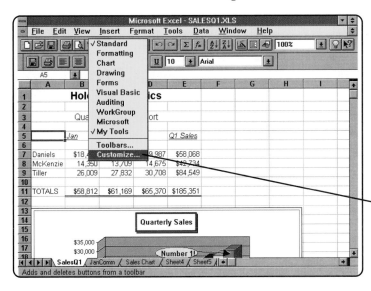

1. **Place** the mouse arrow on the **Standard toolbar**.

2. **Click** the **right mouse button**. A pop-down menu will appear.

3. **Click** on **Customize**. **Release** the mouse button. The Customize dialog box will appear.

4. Click on the **Save button** on the Standard toolbar. It will appear to be recessed.

5. Press and hold the mouse button as you **drag** the button outline to the **Customize dialog box**.

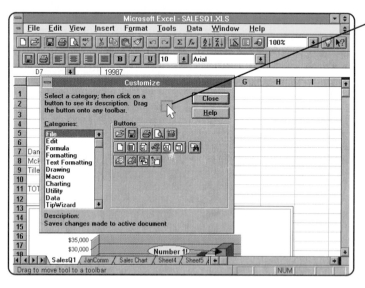

6. Release the mouse button anywhere in the dialog box. The Save button will disappear from the Standard toolbar.

Notice that the Save button is gone from the Standard toolbar.

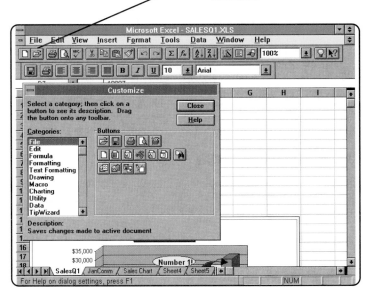

7. **Repeat steps 5 through 7** to remove each of the following:

Print button

Format Painter button

Tip Wizard button

Help button

8. **Click** on **Close** when you have finished removing the buttons. The worksheet and chart will reappear.

MAKING BUTTONS BIGGER

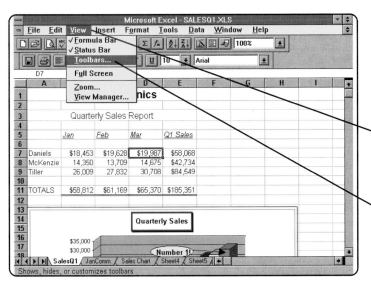

For those of us with bifocals, the ultimate worksheet has larger buttons. Here's how you make buttons larger:

1. **Click** on **View** in the menu bar. A pull-down menu will appear.

2. **Click** on **Toolbars**. The Toolbars dialog box will appear.

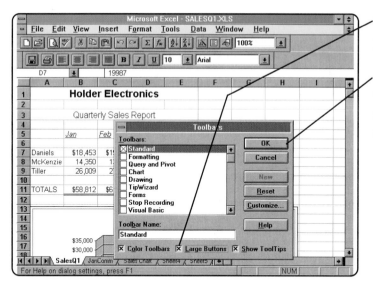

3. Click on **Large Buttons** to put an X in the box.

4. Click on **OK**. The worksheet and chart will reappear with buttons you can actually see! Wow!

DELETING THE CUSTOM TOOLBAR

1. Click on **View** in the menu bar. A pull-down menu will appear.

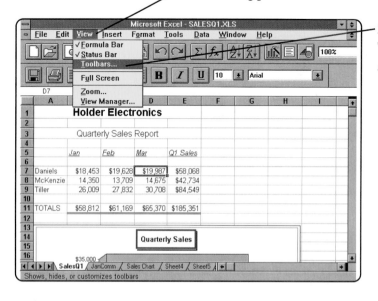

2. Click on **Toolbars**. The Toolbars dialog box will appear.

3. Click on the ⬇ to scroll down to My Tools in the Toolbars at the bottom of the list box.

4. Click on **My Tools** to highlight it.

5. Click on **Delete**. A Microsoft Excel dialog box will appear.

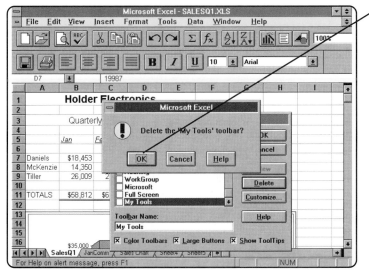

6. Click on **OK**. The Toolbar dialog box will appear in the foreground. The My Tools toolbar will disappear.

RESTORING THE STANDARD AND FORMATTING TOOLBARS

1. **Click repeatedly** on the ⬆ to scroll up to the top of the toolbars list box.

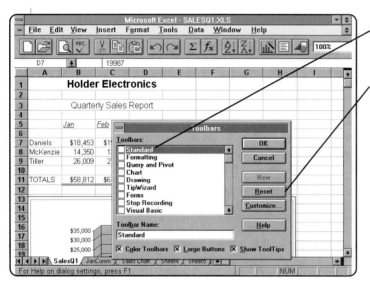

2. **Click** on **Standard** to highlight it.

3. **Click** on **Reset**.

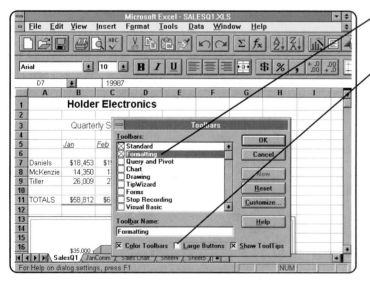

4. **Click** on **Formatting** to place an X in the box.

5. **Click** on **Large buttons** to remove the X from the box.

6. **Click** on **OK**. The Standard and Formatting toolbars will be restored with the original buttons and in their original size.

Protecting Your Work

Excel offers many options in the way you can restrict access to a workbook or its contents. You can prevent others from opening or accessing a workbook. Or you can allow people to open your workbooks but prevent them from saving any changes. By using different passwords, you can even mix the kinds of protection you use in a single workbook so that different groups of people have different levels of access. Just make sure that you can remember each password (or write them down and file them in a safe place)! In this chapter, you will do the following:

❖ Assign password protection to a workbook
❖ Test a password
❖ Remove a password
❖ Assign a password to keep the original file intact
❖ Protect a single worksheet in a workbook
❖ Remove a password from a single worksheet

ASSIGNING PASSWORD PROTECTION TO A WORKBOOK

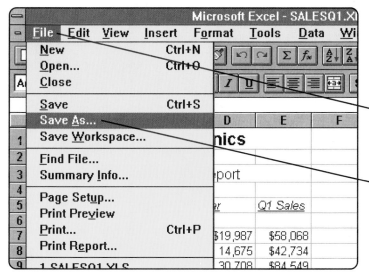

In this section, you will add a password to a workbook so that the workbook cannot be opened without it.

1. **Click** on **File** in the menu bar. The pull-down menu will appear.

2. **Click** on **Save As**. The Save As dialog box will appear.

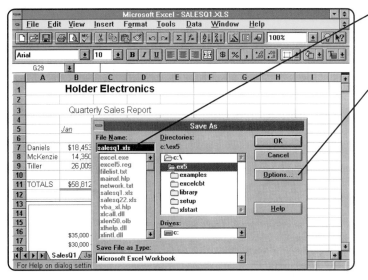

Confirm that the file you want to protect is listed in the File Name box.

3. **Click** on **Options**. The Save Options dialog box will appear.

4. **Type a password** in the **Protection Password box**. Each letter or number you type will show as an asterisk (*). A password can include as many as 15 characters in any combination. The password feature is case-sensitive, so if you use a combination of upper- and lowercase letters, you must remember the exact combination.

WARNING: If you forget your password, you are in deep fertilizer! You will have to re-create the entire file.

5. **Click** on **OK**. The Confirm Password dialog box will appear.

6. Type the **same password** in the **Reenter Protection Password box**.

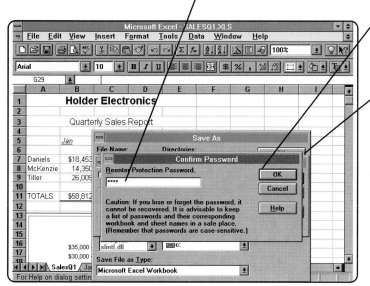

7. Click on **OK**. The Confirm Password dialog box will disappear.

8. Click on **OK** in the Save As dialog box. A Microsoft Excel message box will appear.

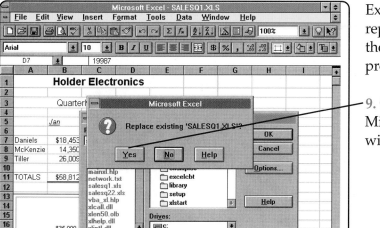

Excel asks if you want to replace the existing file with the one you have just protected with a password.

9. Click on **Yes**. The Microsoft Excel dialog box will disappear.

TESTING A PASSWORD

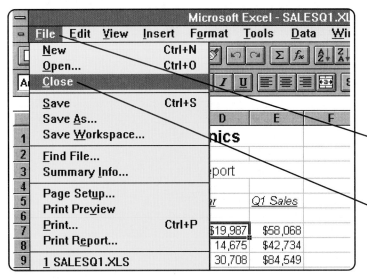

To test whether the password option will prevent unauthorized opening of the workbook, you must close the file and reopen it.

1. Click on **File** in the menu bar. A pull-down menu will appear.

2. Click on **Close**. The SALESQ1.XLS file will disappear and a blank Excel screen will appear.

3. Click on **File** in the menu bar. A pull-down menu will appear.

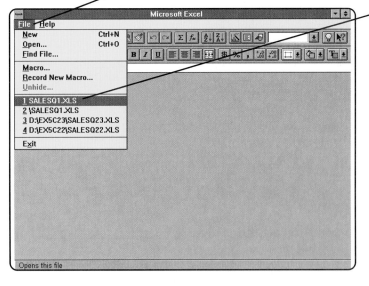

4. Click on **SALESQ1.XLS** to open the file. The Password dialog box will appear.

5. **Type** the password in the **Password text box**.

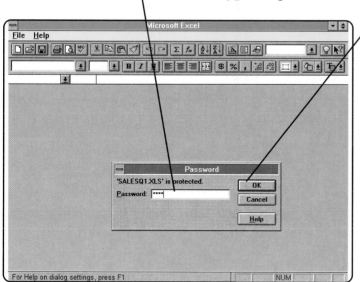

6. **Click** on **OK**. The SALESQ1.XLS worksheet will appear.

REMOVING A PASSWORD

In this section, you will delete the password you added to the workbook in the previous section.

1. **Click** on **File** in the menu bar.

2. **Click** on **Save As**. The Save as dialog box will appear.

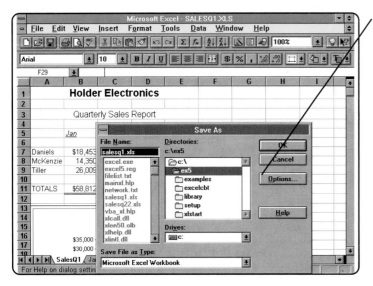

3. Click on **Options**. The Save Options dialog box will appear.

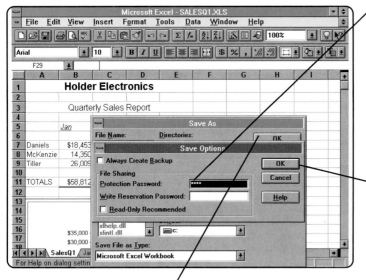

4. Click twice in the **Protection Password box** to highlight the field if it is not already highlighted.

5. Press the **Delete key** on your keyboard to remove the password.

6. Click on **OK**. The Save Options dialog box will disappear and the Save As dialog box will come to the front.

7. Click on **OK** in the Save As dialog box. A Microsoft Excel message box will appear.

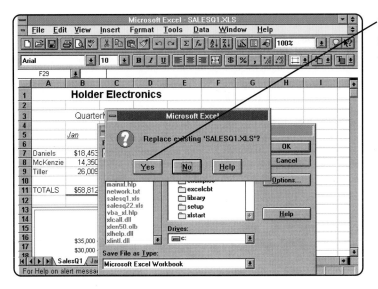

8. **Click** on **Yes**. The SALESQ1.XLS worksheet will appear.

ASSIGNING A PASSWORD TO KEEP THE ORIGINAL FILE INTACT

1. **Repeat steps 1 through 3** in the section "Assigning Password Protection to a Workbook" at the beginning of this chapter to open the Save Options dialog box.

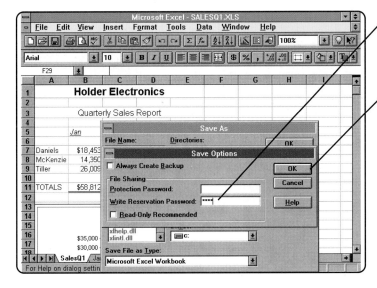

2. **Click** on the **Write Reservation Password box** and **type** a **password**.

3. **Click** on **OK**. The Confirm Password dialog box will appear.

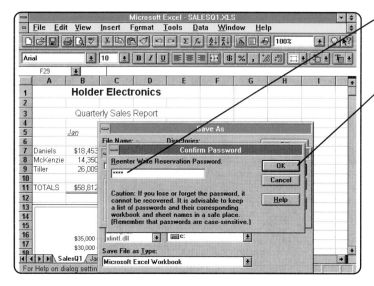

4. Type the **same password** in the **Write Protection Reservation dialog box**.

5. Click on **OK**. The Confirm Password dialog box will disappear.

6. Click on **OK** in the Save As dialog box. A Microsoft Excel message box will appear.

7. Click on **Yes**. The Microsoft Excel dialog box will disappear.

PROTECTING A SINGLE WORKSHEET IN A WORKBOOK

You can allow a person to open a workbook but prevent him or her from making changes in a specific worksheet without the correct password.

1. Click on **Tools** in the menu bar. A pull-down menu will appear.

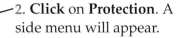

2. Click on **Protection**. A side menu will appear.

3. Click on **Protect Sheet**. The Protect Sheet dialog box will appear.

Notice than an X appears in the squares to the left of "Contents," "Objects," and "Scenarios." Excel has already selected all of the items to be protected. To customize the levels of protection, refer to your *Users Guide*.

4. Type a **password** in the **Password text box**.

5. Click on **OK**. A Confirm Password dialog box will appear.

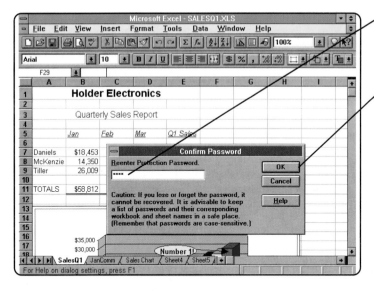

6. **Type** the **same password** in the **Reenter Protection Password dialog box**.

7. **Click** on **OK**. The SALESQ1.XLS file with password-protected worksheets will appear in the window.

REMOVING PASSWORD PROTECTION FROM A WORKSHEET

1. **Click** on **Tools** in the menu bar. The pull-down menu will appear.

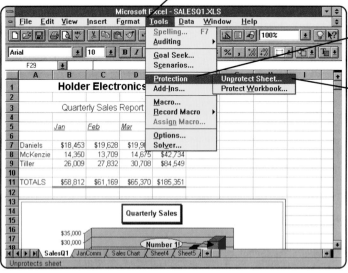

2. **Click** on **Protection**. A side bar will appear.

3. **Click** on **Unprotect Worksheet**. An Unprotect Sheet dialog box will appear.

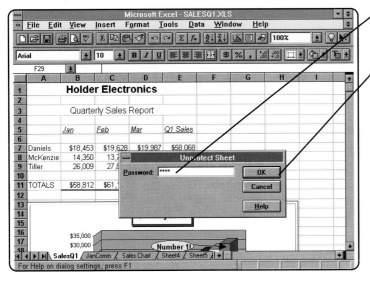

4. **Type** the **password** that protects the sheet.

5. **Click** on **OK**. The dialog box disappears and the sheet is now unprotected.

Converting Another Program's Worksheet to Excel

Excel has made converting a worksheet program a snap. In this chapter, you will do the following:

❖ Open a worksheet from another program and convert it to an Excel for Windows worksheet

❖ Save the converted worksheet as an Excel for Windows file

OPENING A WORKSHEET FROM ANOTHER PROGRAM

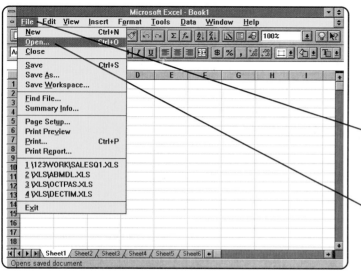

To convert a spreadsheet from another program, such as Lotus 1-2-3, you simply open the file. Excel does the rest!

1. Click on **File** in the menu bar. A pull-down menu will appear.

2. Click on **Open**. The Open File dialog box will appear.

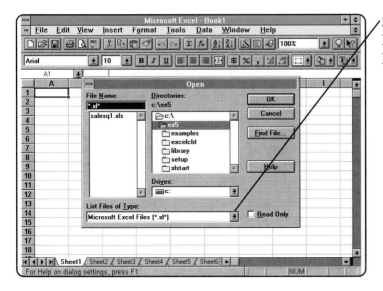

3. **Click** on the ⬇ on the **File text box**. A drop-down list of file types will appear.

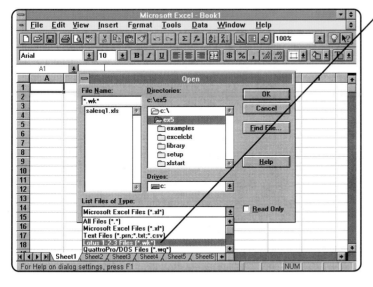

4. **Click** on the **type of file** you want to convert. It will appear in the file type text box. In this example, we are using Lotus 1-2-3 (*.wk*).

5. Click twice on **c:**. A list of all directories on the C drive will appear.

6. Click repeatedly on the ⬇ to scroll down the list of directories until you find the directory that contains the worksheet you want to convert. In this example, the file is the 123work directory.

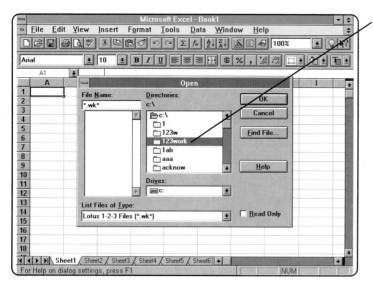

7. Click twice on the **directory name**. The file(s) in the directory will appear in the File Name list box on the left.

8. Click twice on the **file** you want to convert. The File will open.

ADDING SPREADSHEET GRIDLINES

Your spreadsheet may not have all the formatting or formulas still applied when you open it into Excel. In this case the gridlines were turned off. This example will show one way to turn the gridlines back on.

1. Click on **View** in the menu bar. A pull-down menu will appear.

2. Click on **Toolbars**. The Toolbars dialog box will appear.

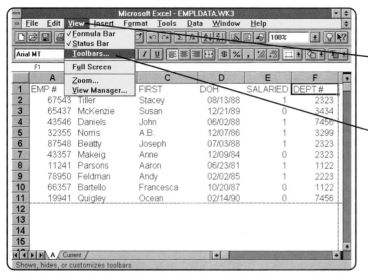

3. **Click** on **Forms** to put an ✕ in the box.

4. **Click** on **OK**. The Toolbars dialog box will disappear and the Forms toolbar will appear on your worksheet.

5. **Click** on the **Toggle Grid button** at the bottom left of the toolbar. After a pause the gridlines will appear.

6. Click on the **Control menu box** (☐) on the Form toolbar to close the Form toolbar.

SAVING A CONVERTED FILE AS AN EXCEL WORKBOOK FILE

1. Click on the **Save button**. The Save As dialog box will appear.

Notice that the 1-2-3 file format is selected in the Save File as Type box.

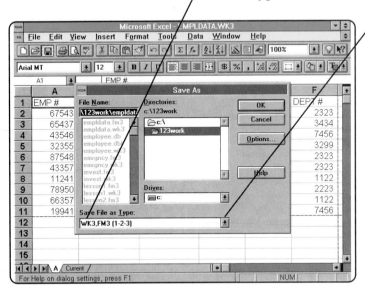

2. Click on the ⬇ next to the Save File as Type box. A drop down list will appear.

3. Drag the **scroll button** up or down the scroll bar until you see Microsoft Excel Workbook.

4. Click on **Microsoft Excel Workbook**.

5. Click on **OK**. You will see the Summary Info dialog box. See "Naming a Workbook" in Chapter 2 if you need help with this dialog box.

Program Manager

Part VI: Appendix

Appendix: Installing Excel 5	Page 244

Installing Excel 5

This appendix will describe a standard (typical) installation for an upgrade to Excel 5. You can also follow these steps if you are installing Excel for the first time. In both instances, however, the installation program will interact with your particular computer. Therefore, you may see slightly different messages or screens than shown in these examples. If you want to customize your installation, refer to the *User's Guide* that came with your software. In this appendix, you will do the following:

❖ Install Excel 5

Before you start, make sure that you have made and are using backup copies of your Excel 5 Install disks. If you need help backing up your disks, see the *User's Guide*.

INSTALLING EXCEL 5 FOR WINDOWS

1. **Open** Windows by **typing win** at the DOS prompt (C:\). The Program Manager opening screen will appear. Your screen may look different from this one.

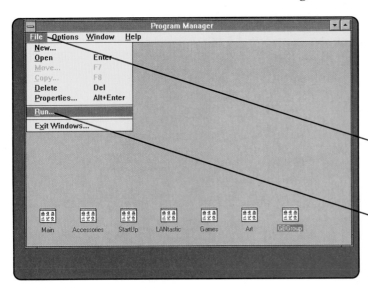

2. **Insert** your **backup copy** of **Excel 5 Disk 1** into drive A (or B).

3. **Click** on **File** in the menu bar. A pull-down menu will appear.

4. **Click** on **Run**. The Run dialog box will appear.

Notice that the cursor is flashing in the Command Line box. When you start typing, your text will be entered in the box.

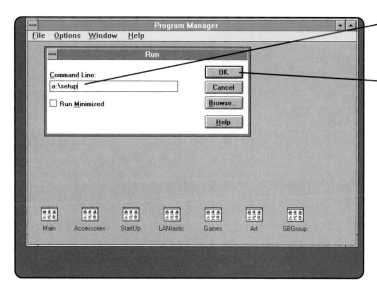

5. **Type A:\setup** (or B:\setup).

6. **Click** on **OK**. The hourglass will appear briefly with a Microsoft Setup message box that says, "Starting Excel Setup, please wait...." Next, the Microsoft Excel 5.0 Setup dialog box will appear.

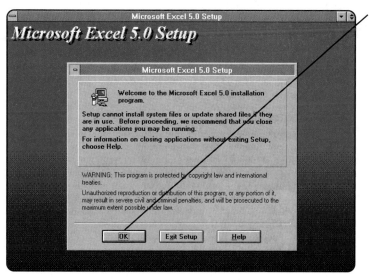

7. **Click** on **OK**.

Notice that the cursor is flashing in the Name text box. When you start typing, it will disappear.

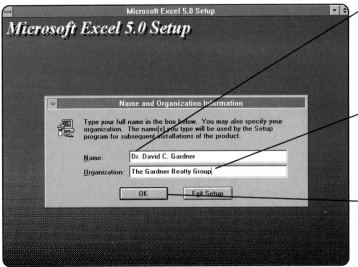

8. Type your **full name** in the Name text box and then **press** the **Tab key** to move the cursor to the Organization text box.

9. Type the name of your **organization**, if applicable, in the Organization text box.

10. **Click** on **OK**. The Confirm Name and Organization Information dialog box will appear.

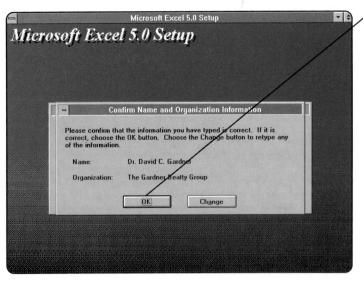

11. Click on **OK** if the information is correct. The Microsoft Excel 5.0 Setup dialog box concerning your Serial number will appear.

If the information is not correct, **click** on **No**. The previous dialog box will appear. After making your corrections, **click** on **OK** (see step 10) to return to this dialog box and complete step 11.

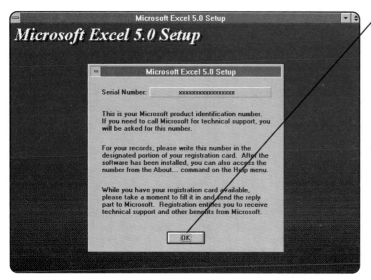

12. Click on **OK**. An Excel 5.0 message box will appear that says, "Setup is searching for installed components." Then a Microsoft Excel 5.0 Setup dialog box will appear concerning the directory where the Excel 5.0 files will be placed.

13. Click on **Continue**.

If you have other versions of Excel you might want to put Excel 5 in a different directory to keep it separate from previous versions, otherwise Excel 5 will write over the old version. If you do not have another version of Excel on your machine skip to step 18.

14. Click on **Change Directory**.

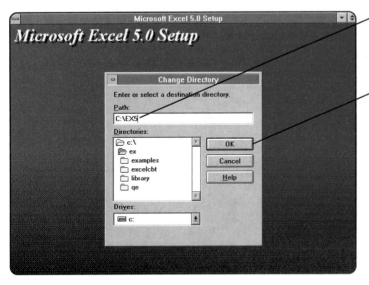

15. Type C:\EX5 (or the directory name of your choice).

16. Click on **OK**. A Microsoft Excel 5.0 Setup dialog box will appear.

17. **Confirm** the destination directory is C:\EX5 (or the name you selected).

18. **Click** on **Yes**. The Microsoft Excel 5.0 Setup dialog box prompting you for the correct directory will appear.

19. **Click** on **OK**.

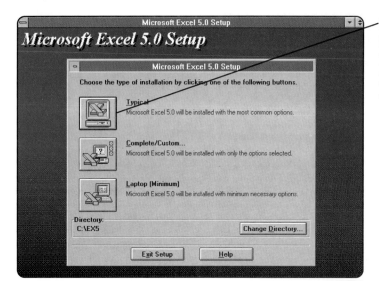

20. **Click** on the **Typical button**. After a pause the Microsoft Excel 5.0 Choose Program Group dialog box will appear.

You can select an existing program group if you do not want a separate Excel group icon. Click on the name of the program group where you would like Excel to put the program item icons. Otherwise, Excel will create a separate Group icon called Microsoft. In this example, it will be Microsoft Office.

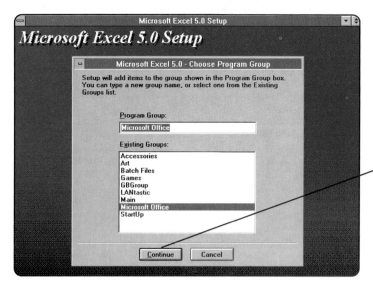

21. **Click** on **Continue**. A Microsoft Excel 5 setup message box will appear saying "Setup is checking for necessary disk space".

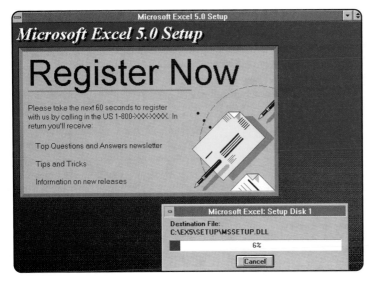

At this point sit back and relax. Excel will now begin copying the files from the disks to your hard drive. The Microsoft Excel 5.0 dialog box will show you the percentage of completion in copying files from the disk in drive A (or B).

After Excel is done copying the files from Disk 1 another Microsoft Excel 5.0 Setup message will appear.

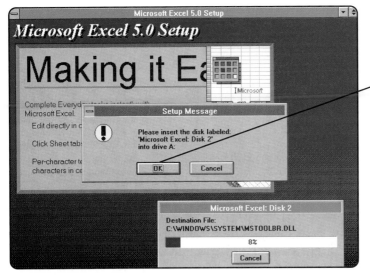

22. **Remove Disk 1** from Drive A (or B) and **insert Disk 2**.

23. **Click** on **OK**. Excel will begin copying the files on Disk 2.

Once again the Microsoft Excel dialog box will show you the percent of progress.

24. **Repeat steps 22 and 23 for the remaining disks. This will take a while so be patient!**

25. **Click** on **OK**.

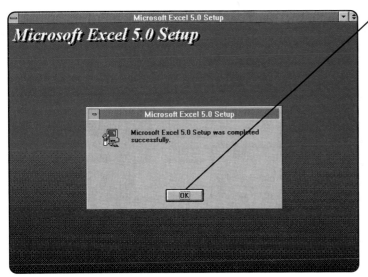

26. **Click** on **OK**. The Excel Microsoft Office Program group window will appear. It may appear in a different size or location than the one shown here.

Congratulations! You have successfully installed Excel 5.0.

At this point reboot your computer and go to the "Introduction" at the beginning of this book. Select your first learning goal and have fun.

Go to step 3 in Chapter 1, "Setting Up a New Work-sheet," to start with a screen that looks like this one.

Index

D